# Praise for *Business Innovation and Disruptive Technology*

"In this economic environment, true leaders will continue to use emerging technologies to improve their businesses. Nick's book provides a platform to consider the business implications for key emerging technologies."

—*Mark Sherman, General Partner, Battery Ventures*

"The author gives a deep and valuable presentation of the basic strategic and business aspects of various emerging technologies. These so-called 'disruptive' technologies can contribute in a significant way to the development of new business models in many different industries and, generally speaking, can start the 'round two of the Internet era.'"

—*Mauro Sentinelli, Managing Director, Telecom Italia Mobile*

"*Business Innovation and Disruptive Technology* is a great read for anyone who wants to understand current trends and the underlying value of today's most important evolutionary, revolutionary, and disruptive technologies."

—*Chris O'Neill, General Partner, Vortex Partners*

# Business Innovation and Disruptive Technology

## Harnessing the Power of Breakthrough Technology
### ... for Competitive Advantage

ISBN 0-13-047397-9

90000

9 780130 473974

**FINANCIAL TIMES**

Prentice Hall

In an increasingly competitive world, it is quality
of thinking that gives an edge—an idea that opens new
doors, a technique that solves a problem, or an insight
that simply helps make sense of it all.

We work with leading authors in the various arenas
of business and finance to bring cutting-edge thinking
and best learning practice to a global market.

It is our goal to create world-class print publications
and electronic products that give readers
knowledge and understanding which can then be
applied, whether studying or at work.

To find out more about our business
products, you can visit us at www.ft-ph.com

Pearson
Education

# Business Innovation and Disruptive Technology

Harnessing the Power of Breakthrough Technology ... for Competitive Advantage

Nicholas D. Evans

An Imprint of PEARSON EDUCATION

Upper Saddle River, NJ • New York • London • San Francisco • Toronto
Sydney • Tokyo • Singapore • Hong Kong • Cape Town
Madrid • Paris • Milan • Munich • Amsterdam
**www.ft-ph.com**

A Cataloging-in-Publication data record for this book can be obtained from the Library of Congress.

Editorial/Production Supervision: *Carol Moran*
Cover design director: *Jerry Votta*
Cover design: *Nina Scuderi*
Art Director: *Gail Cocker-Bogusz*
Interior design: *Meg VanArsdale*
Manufacturing buyer: *Maura Zaldivar*
Executive editor: *Jim Boyd*
Editorial assistant: *Allyson Kloss*
Marketing manager: *Bryan Gambrel*

©2003 Pearson Education, Inc.
Publishing as Financial Times Prentice Hall
Upper Saddle River, New Jersey 07458

Financial Times Prentice Hall books are widely used by corporations and government agencies for training, marketing, and resale.

For information regarding corporate and government bulk discounts please contact:
Corporate and Government Sales (800) 382-3419 or corpsales@pearsontechgroup.com.

Company and product names mentioned herein are the trademarks or registered trademarks of their respective owners.

Printed in the United States of America

10  9  8  7  6  5  4  3  2  1

ISBN 0-13-047397-9

Pearson Education Ltd.
Pearson Education Australia Pty, Limited
Pearson Education Singapore, Pte. Ltd.
Pearson Education North Asia Ltd.
Pearson Education Canada, Ltd.
Pearson Educación de Mexico, S.A. de C.V.
Pearson Education—Japan
Pearson Education Malaysia, Pte. Ltd.

# FINANCIAL TIMES PRENTICE HALL BOOKS

*For more information, please go to www.ft-ph.com*

Dr. Judith M. Bardwick
*Seeking the Calm in the Storm: Managing Chaos in Your Business Life*

Thomas L. Barton, William G. Shenkir, and Paul L. Walker
*Making Enterprise Risk Management Pay Off:
How Leading Companies Implement Risk Management*

Michael Basch
*CustomerCulture: How FedEx and Other Great Companies Put the
Customer First Every Day*

J. Stewart Black and Hal B. Gregersen
*Leading Strategic Change: Breaking Through the Brain Barrier*

Deirdre Breakenridge
*Cyberbranding: Brand Building in the Digital Economy*

William C. Byham, Audrey B. Smith, and Matthew J. Paese
*Grow Your Own Leaders: How to Identify, Develop, and Retain
Leadership Talent*

Jonathan Cagan and Craig M. Vogel
*Creating Breakthrough Products: Innovation from Product Planning
to Program Approval*

Subir Chowdhury
*The Talent Era: Achieving a High Return on Talent*

Sherry Cooper
*Ride the Wave: Taking Control in a Turbulent Financial Age*

James W. Cortada
*21st Century Business: Managing and Working
in the New Digital Economy*

James W. Cortada
*Making the Information Society: Experience, Consequences,
and Possibilities*

Aswath Damodaran
*The Dark Side of Valuation: Valuing Old Tech, New Tech,
and New Economy Companies*

Henry A. Davis and William W. Sihler
*Financial Turnarounds: Preserving Enterprise Value*

# Contents

# 4   Real-Time Computing   87

# 5   Business Process Management   109

# 6  Mobile Business  123

# 7  Enterprise Security  143

# 8  Emerging Technology Strategic Roadmap  161

# 9 Future Trends   175

# 10 Conclusion   197

# References   201

# Index   207

# About the Author

# Foreword

The internet "tsunami" has forever accelerated the pace of infusion of technology discontinuities into the corporate workplace. While many firms grasp this trend, relatively few have been able to take action and optimize corporate (enterprise) processes to take full advantage of emerging technologies. *Business Innovation and Disruptive Technology* is a very important work that will guide corporate decision makers through the maze of emerging technologies and, even more importantly, will help firms distance themselves from the competition and monetize the benefits of these technologies.

As a 20-plus-year aerospace industry executive, I can personally attest that the use of a radar metaphor in *Business Innovation and Disruptive Technology* is extremely applicable and appropriate. If the speed of your targets (i.e., emerging technologies) is faster than your ability to react to intercept these targets (i.e., detection, classification, and decision making) then the consequences are extremely negative (i.e., loss of competitiveness). Reciprocally, if you have a robust radar system, you will be in an advantageous competitive position. Mr. Evans's work will allow you to create a robust enterprise-emerging technology radar system.

I have known Mr. Evans for some time, and he has developed a keen perspective on emerging technologies and their associated implementation. He presents a coherent, synthesized viewpoint, simultaneously viewing the world of emerging technology and associated implementation challenges through the lens of a pragmatic technologist and an enterprise consultant.

Mr. Evans combines a deep understanding of these complex topics with an easy-to-understand format, which makes *Business Innovation and Disruptive Technology* a must read for cutting edge executives wishing to take a proactive approach to emerging technology evaluation and implementation.

Charles Marinello
*Strategy Director*
*Texas Instruments, Inc.*
*May 20, 2002*

# Acknowledgments

This book owes a great deal of thanks to the people who have inspired me in the world of emerging and disruptive technologies and to the academics, executives, and venture capitalists, some old friends and some new acquaintances, who have expressed interest and enthusiasm for this project.

In particular, I'd like to thank (in alphabetical order by company): Mark Sherman (Battery Ventures), Ann Kelly (Bowstreet), Catherine Marchand (DuPont Performance Coatings), Matthew Bowers (Incucomm), Ray Lane (Kleiner Perkins Caufield & Byers), Bill Barhydt and Sally Khudairi (KnowNow), David Dickinson (Nokia), Charles Marinello (Texas Instruments), Don Hicks (University of Texas at Dallas), and Chris O'Neill (Vortex Partners).

I'd like to thank Jim Boyd, Executive Editor at Financial Times Prentice Hall, for his interest in bringing yet another idea to fruition and for our always enjoyable conversations. I'd also like to thank Carol Moran for her great work on the production side.

Finally, I'd like to thank my wife, Michele, and my sons, Andrew and David, for their patience with me and for allowing me to take family time on evenings and weekends in order to put this book together. Without their encouragement and support, this book would not have been possible.

> Readers who would like to correspond with the author
> can contact him at *ndevans@hotmail.com.*

# Introduction

*"We ought not be over-anxious to encourage innovation, in case of doubtful improvement, for an old system must ever have two advantages over a new one; it is established and it is understood."*

—C.C. Colton

## The Case for Emerging and Disruptive Technologies

This book is designed to be a handbook for executives who want to gain the latest insights and strategies for identifying and leveraging emerging and disruptive technologies in the software arena for "back to basics" enterprise value creation, competitive advantage, and increased business agility within their organization.

Traditionally, leverage of emerging technology has been the exclusive domain of businesses that are seen as pioneers and early adopters—not of the mainstream. Mainstream business has historically waited and cautiously observed the results of others before taking the plunge themselves. However, in today's economic and competitive climate, and in light of recent world events which have required increased focus on resiliency and security, it becomes mandatory for mainstream business to rethink its strategy around the exploitation of these emerging and disruptive technologies.

The strategic use of technology within the enterprise is no longer just an issue for the chief information officer (CIO) or chief technology officer (CTO). Business spending on technology is such a large part of corporate capital and ongoing expenditure that all business executives, including the CEO and board members, need to have a clear understanding of how it can be most effectively leveraged and exploited within their organization. This is an increasingly difficult task due to the vacuum that has been created in the technology roadmap after the Internet boom-and-bust cycle of the last several years. What seemed a clear path just a few years or even a few months ago is now a minefield of potential distractions; technologies are looking for business problems to solve like a hammer looking for a nail. Emerging and disruptive technologies that can have a real impact are out there, but they will require a proactive approach on the part of the business in order to identify and implement them. The noise level and risk level are now simply too high to take a passive approach or to implement everything that comes into view for fear of being beaten by the competition.

Today, businesses need to extend their radar, both to protect existing assets and to build for the future by leveraging emerging technology as a growth engine. As this book aims to show, certain emerging and disruptive technologies, in the right combination, can become the strategic weapon for both offense and defense in the business world of the new millennium.

Thus, determining which emerging technologies, beyond the previous wave of e-business applications, have the potential for increasing business productivity and even the productivity of the overall economy is something that is on the minds of many executives. Executives need to know how emerging technology in the enterprise software arena can benefit their business in today's "back-to-basics" environment. They want to know how they can increase shareholder value, increase customer satisfaction and loyalty, increase revenues, improve productivity, and reduce costs. They also need to know which technologies to invest in, where these technologies are heading and how they can be applied to their unique industries and business processes, and how to avoid the many pitfalls along the way. In these times when "back-to-basics" is a corporate mantra, executives also need to ensure that they manage risk and focus on solid return on investment for all information technology (IT) initiatives both on the current radar screen and beyond.

# Our Agenda

In this book we approach emerging and disruptive technologies not only as the next business differentiator and source of competitive advantage but also as the next source of solid business value for enterprise operations. We will make recommendations on how to identify and exploit these technologies to design more competitive and agile companies and markets.

The book covers the strategy, process, and technology aspects behind some of today's most promising emerging technologies with a focus on how to achieve real-world results that benefit the top and bottom line for an organization. One of the goals of this book is to help executives maximize their value from these technologies, to reshape their business, not just their business processes. The stakes are a lot higher now than they were in the mid- and late nineties when we saw large investments in enterprise resource planning (ERP) implementations, millennium bug fixes, and dot-com initiatives with arguably less scrutiny on investments than is true today. The packaged applications that have been implemented over the past several years have provided a good first wave of business value, but it is now important for businesses to optimize those investments by adding unique extensions and differentiators. Investments in IT must have a stronger payback in terms of the business value extracted, and it is critical that business and IT executives work even more closely together toward corporate objectives.

Innovations in existing software categories and the emergence of entirely new categories have created tremendous opportunity for businesses to re-engineer and rethink their IT applications and processes. Some of the emerging technologies covered in this book include enterprise software categories such as Web services, peer services, business process management, real-time computing, mobile business, and enterprise security. Additionally, we explore trends and advances in areas such as software as a service, grid computing, computing on demand, devices and sensors, electronic tagging, artificial intelligence, speech technologies, and new forms of visual interfaces. The potential impact of these technologies over the next several years will range from simply reshaping business processes to reshaping entire industries.

Much has been published on the technical details of these emerging technologies, such as Web services, but for the business executive the implications and benefits are unclear, at best.

Collectively, these technologies represent the next generation of the Internet. It is vital that business executives gain an understanding of how they may be applied within their enterprise for competitive advantage. The business must now extend its radar since these emerging and disruptive technologies *are* the next competitive edge.

Packaged applications can take us only so far. It is this new wave of enabling technologies that will set businesses apart. The challenge is that these technologies do not create the value themselves. It is all about execution—how these technologies are identified, combined, and implemented will be the keys to success. There is also no single "magic bullet"—no one single technology will provide the solution, but their combination will yield tremendous synergies.

# Our Approach

*Business Innovation and Disruptive Technology* begins with an overview of the trends within the enterprise, on both the business and information technology side and within the software industry, that are driving us toward the need to extend the radar. Within the business world, there is increased uncertainty in terms of future growth predictions and the direction of the economy. Businesses are adopting a back-to-basics approach focusing on cost takeout and performance improvement. Information technology departments are increasingly called upon to justify every penny they spend and to do more with less. The software industry is undergoing its own transformation. The software-as-a-service movement, where software is moved to the network for others to subscribe to or rent, is changing the business models for almost all of these companies. It is changing the way that software is planned, designed, constructed, delivered, and maintained. Many emerging infrastructure technologies such as Web services and peer-to-peer computing have enabled new business possibilities in terms of redefining how business value can be delivered or extracted. Many of the technologies have reached a trigger point where they are primed for mass market adoption due to reduced costs and standardization.

Chapter 1 starts with a discussion of the trends within the business and software communities. The book then goes into detail for each of the major emerging and disruptive technology categories that are profiled. Chapters 2 through 7 cover Web services, peer services, real-time computing, business process management, mobile business, and enterprise security, respectively. The descriptions of each of these emerging technologies and critical disciplines are tackled from the business perspective. The book focuses on the business scenarios to which these technologies can be applied and the corresponding benefits that can be realized. Brief technical descriptions of the technologies are included in order to help business leaders understand the underlying infrastructure that is required to be put into place and the conceptual models around how the software interacts. The book then goes on to provide industry examples of success stories and covers some of the leading and emerging software companies within each category, both public and private. Industry examples are taken from a variety of major corporations in verticals, including communications and content, consumer and industrial products, financial services, health care, high-tech, and government. After coverage of the value proposition of the specific technology in terms of business scenarios and strengths and weaknesses, each chapter concludes by making strategy recommendations for how to exploit these technologies and calculate return on investment.

In Chapter 8 we look at how organizations should approach their emerging and disruptive technology strategy and how processes can be put into place in order to identify and implement these solutions, to manage risk, and to maximize the return on investment. This chapter raises the strategy discussion from the earlier focus on exploiting individual emerging technologies to a corporate level discussion on how to extend the radar across the organization.

In Chapter 9 we look at some of the future trends in computing that have relevance to business stakeholders. We look at where information technology is headed and how we may interact with computers in the future. These trends include innovations in core computing and networks, devices and sensors, and user interfaces and human–computer interaction. As software moves out to the network and becomes a readily available service, we are seeing the rise of information technology as a utility much like the water, gas, telephone, and electric utilities. In fact, companies are already exploring the potential of delivering information over the public power network as discussed in our section on power line networking. The section on grid computing and computing on demand explores the opportunities that are possible by tapping into the collective power of the Internet operating system and by accessing computing resources on an as-needed basis. As chips and sensors are embedded into everyday devices, we are entering an era of ubiquitous computing where there is not only human-to-machine interaction but also machine-to-machine interaction and object-to-object interaction. The chapter also covers the innovations in user interfaces and human–computer interaction with coverage of new applications in artificial intelligence, new speech technologies, and new forms of interactions via multimodal and visual interfaces.

In Chapter 10 we look at our current position in the long-term evolution of the Internet and of electronic business applications. Having spent the past five years or so learning what works and what doesn't work, we will spend the next five years realizing the productivity and value that were anticipated when we first embarked on the journey.

# 1

# The Need for Enterprise Innovation

*"Computing is rapidly approaching an inflection point where science fiction writers' predictions of helpful, ubiquitous and seamless technology will become a reality."*

—Richard Rashid, Senior Vice President, Microsoft Research

U nderlying trends both within the business world and the software industry are driving us toward the need to extend the radar, to focus on emerging and disruptive technologies as the next source for growth and competitive advantage within the enterprise.

In fact, the need to extend the radar for competitive advantage will cause mainstream businesses to become more like the pioneers and early adopters of technology innovation. Over time, this may even reshape the classical technology adoption lifecycle—the current model for how businesses adopt new technologies. Rather than following the bell-shaped curve with the "chasm" or delay in adoption between the pioneers and early adopters and the mainstream business, the chasm will be pushed later down the curve between the mainstream business and the laggards. By extending the radar and acting on those radar signals as an early warning system, the mainstream business will effectively pull itself into the domain of the pioneers and early adopters and be able to gain the same level of competitive advantage by acting not necessarily as a first mover but as a smart mover.

This smart-mover approach will require much more than simply evaluating and implementing new software or "me too"-style technology adoption. It will require the mainstream business to rethink how it identifies and prioritizes emerging and disruptive technologies and how it applies them. It will require changes within both information technology departments and within business units in order to intelligently apply the right technologies to the right business challenges and opportunities at the right time.

In addition to looking at the trends and changes within the business world and within the software industry, we'll also take an advance look at some of the key application areas where these technologies can be applied, and at some of the key vendors who provide these solutions and hold the keys to the enabling technologies of the future. The software industry is transforming itself by moving from packaged software products to software as a service on the network. This transformation will have a profound effect on both the software industry itself and on many industries who rely on software for the delivery and exchange of value with employees, customers, and business partners.

## Business and IT Trends

General trends within the corporate enterprise, on both the business and information technology sides, are numerous. On the business side, they have included increased uncertainty in terms of future business scenarios and economic outlook, an emphasis on "back-to-basics" operations for cost reduction and productivity enhancements, and a focus on improved business resiliency via the application of enhanced security. On the information technology side, there has been a focus on improved business management of IT in order to extract the most value from existing resources, and a general realignment of business and IT priorities from those of previous years.

Today's businesses are focused on defending and safeguarding their existing market positions in addition to targeting market growth. Cost-constrained businesses are generally focused on achieving more from the same amount of resources in terms of people, knowledge, and systems, and in optimizing their existing operations and business processes. As an example, within the supply chain, businesses are attempting to optimize their interactions with other supply chain participants in order to increase visibility of information and transactions and reduce the "bull-whip" effect on inventory due to changes in supply and demand. Any new initiatives have to have strong business cases in terms of the return on investment and the short-term and long-term benefits.

## Increased Uncertainty

More than anything else, the year 2002 and beyond represent an age of increased uncertainty in the global business and economic arena. In the current economic climate and in light of recent world events, companies are focusing on a back-to-basics approach where the major emphasis is on taking care of existing customers, increasing resiliency of operations, and controlling costs within the enterprise. In addition, many businesses are focused on survival rather than expansion. Companies are trying to optimize their returns from investments in existing assets and resources rather than placing huge amounts of new investment in the "next big thing." All this means, at least in the short term, that new initiatives need to be very carefully planned and executed and a smaller number will be funded in the upcoming years than has been the case over the past three or four years.

Due to this increased uncertainty, businesses are proceeding cautiously and monitoring events both internally and externally. The vacuum created by the lull in business activity has created an excellent window of opportunity for businesses to reassess and realign priorities and strategic plans for moving forward. Even analyst firms are advising business clients to plan for multiple scenarios including best-case and worst-case outlooks for their business over the next 12 to 24 months.

## Productivity

One of the many debates around technology in the business community has been the question of the extent to which technology has actually improved productivity, both within individual businesses and on a macroeconomic basis. An important point to bear in mind is that new technology affects the economy only when it has been broadly adopted and utilized. For example, the innovations in electric power took 40 years, from the 1880s to the 1920s, to be fully realized and leveraged effectively by businesses. Computing technologies have been with us since the 1950s, but it has been only within the last two decades that these innovations have been fully leveraged within the business sector in the form of networking technologies, low cost personal computers and servers, and enterprise software. Internet technologies, while with us since the 1970s in the form of networking protocols, have been fully adopted by the business community only over the past five years. Thus, in the software sector, we can expect the next 20 years to be just as eventful as the last, if not more so, as we enter an era where computing moves into everyday objects via embedded chips such as radio frequency identification (RFID) tags, and software becomes truly pervasive in our society.

Despite the fact that these are early days for the software industry, the U.S. economy has seen considerable increases in productivity over the past decade that have corresponded with increased investments in technology. According to the U.S. Bureau of Labor Statistics, nonfarm business productivity, measured in terms of output per hour, has grown by an average of 2.7 percent each year from 1995 to 2000. There are still substantial productivity improvements to be gained as computing becomes ever more pervasive. It is estimated that the adoption of computing into everyday objects such as consumer and industrial products will create a total savings of $70 billion in the United States and $155 billion internationally. The cost savings will come from areas such as improved visibility into the supply chain, theft reduction, and improved operations.

## Security

On the security front, companies are reassessing their exposure and performing risk assessments to uncover vulnerabilities. Once risk assessments have been conducted, companies can formulate appropriate strategies to implement the required processes and procedures in order to safeguard their people, physical assets, and IT systems. The events of recent cyber-attacks and even of September 11th have meant that the cost/benefit equation for enterprise security has been forever altered. The risks are much higher and enterprises must now invest larger sums in order to protect themselves as much as possible from the consequences of a variety of natural and man-made disasters. Of course, it is impossible to have complete security, and the costs to even approach this limit are astronomical, but enterprises can invest enough to give themselves an adequate level of protection for most common scenarios based upon the degree of risk they can tolerate.

Business disruption can not only cause problems in communications and business activities, it can also adversely affect a company's stock price and reputation with customers and suppliers. It is now more important than ever for companies to have well-rehearsed and frequently updated processes and procedures to account for a variety of adverse scenarios. These may include Internet email and denial-of-service attacks from worms and viruses, physical attacks on property, loss of communications, loss of documents, and information theft. With companies increasingly opening up their networks and applications to customers, partners and suppliers, and using an ever more diverse set of computing devices and networks, it is important to have the appropriate levels of authentication, access control, and encryption in place. These three forms of security help to ensure that only authorized individuals can gain access to the corporate network, that they have access to only those applications for which they are entitled, and that information cannot be understood and altered while in transit. In Chapter 7, we take a detailed look at some of the new techniques for authentication, access control, and encryption, including a number of biometric authentication systems and intrusion detection systems. We also look at security from the perspective of prevention, detection, and reaction.

## Business Management of IT

Business executives and chief information officers are also placing more emphasis on the business management of information technology i.e., placing more controls on how information technology departments are managed and which initiatives get funded. With large percentages of organizations' capital and recurring expenditures going into computing infrastructure and applications, information technology departments are increasingly required to justify each and every investment and maximize their returns. During the last half of the 1990s, U.S. corporations spent an average of $365 billion a year on technology, about 70 percent more than in the first half of the decade.

To run IT departments like businesses, chief information officers need to know what they have in place already in terms of people and technology resources, and they need to minimize their cost of ownership. They need to understand usage patterns to determine how existing applications are being utilized and the value that is being extracted on an ongoing basis. They also need to be aware of underutilized assets and to develop strategies for improving their utilization and overall effectiveness across the corporation.

Keeping track of IT assets is becoming increasingly difficult as the number and variety of computing devices and applications proliferate. Employees now utilize a variety of devices including personal computers, laptops, personal digital assistants, cell phones, and pagers. Many of these are owned by employees themselves, but as these devices are standardized upon and become corporate-issued tools for mobile employees, they need to be carefully secured, controlled, and managed. Devices must be accurately inventoried and their usage patterns need to be tracked in order to report on the total cost of computing and return on investment for various application initiatives.

Companies such as mFormation Technologies provide wireless infrastructure management software to control and manage rapidly growing worldwide populations of wireless users, applications, and devices. Their *Enterprise Manager* software product helps companies maintain an up-to-date view of their wireless assets and how they are being used. It includes end-to-end, real-time performance management and fault localization capabilities to enable help desk and IT support staff to quickly pinpoint and resolve user, network, and device problems. This type of solution represents the next generation of software that we can expect to see in the infrastructure management space. It brings the same level of management to wireless infrastructure as IT departments have over the rest of their IT infrastructure. As the business management of IT becomes more of a discipline, these vendors will help to provide the tools necessary for IT staff to get a handle on their infrastructure and manage resources on a real-time basis.

## IT Priorities

As business priorities change, information technology priorities are being changed accordingly. An *Internet Week* survey of 268 IT managers, shown in Table 1-1, found that the top e-business priorities for 2002 were improving customer service and reducing costs. Other priorities included increasing online sales to business customers, improving online communications with suppliers, developing and expanding electronic supply chains, and developing new Internet sales channels. The survey also found that 42 percent of participants stated that their top management was willing to invest in e-business but was more skeptical and scrupulous about return on investment.

Table 1-1    Companies' Top E-Business Priorities for 2002. Source: *Internet Week*.

| Rank | Feature | Percentage |
|------|---------|-----------|
| 1 | Improving customer service | 68% |
| 2 | Reducing costs | 60% |
| 3 | Increasing online sales to business customers | 24% |
| 4 | Improving online communications with suppliers | 24% |
| 5 | Developing/expanding electronic supply chain | 21% |
| 6 | Developing new Internet sales channels | 21% |
| 7 | Increasing market share via the Web | 20% |
| 8 | Launching/expanding online procurement | 19% |
| 9 | Increasing online sales to consumers | 18% |
| 10 | Participating in an Internet exchange | 11% |
| 11 | Other | 15% |

According to the same *Internet Week* survey, the main challenges facing companies' e-business efforts included cost and tight budgets, security, measuring return on investment, Web-to-legacy integration, data and content management, customer or partner resistance, and complexity of technology. The most important group targeted for e-business initiatives in 2002 were customers at 67 percent, followed by internal employees at 17 percent, and suppliers and dealers/resellers both at eight percent, according to the survey. Information technology priorities undoubtedly will change from year to year or even from month to month, but the numbers help to illustrate the renewed focus on the basics such as improving customer service and reducing costs.

## Emerging Technology as the Next Competitive Advantage

Within this context of the back-to-basics approach, emerging technologies can be applied as an enabler of cost reduction, increased resiliency and security, and competitive advantage. They can be applied within the business for both offense and defense. Emerging technologies provide new ways to deliver value and can dramatically reshape business processes. Disruptive technologies can reshape entire industries. They effectively allow us to rewrite the rule book and define new forms of value creation and value exchange. They can empower corporate planners and strategists to go beyond traditional, linear business development strategies and to explore new directions and new business models for their organizations. Despite the demise of the dot-com economy, software is the main engine for innovation across almost all business processes from design and production to fulfillment. The bursting of the dot-com bubble merely illustrated that not all businesses can be executed in terms of pure-play dot-com models. Moreover, the Internet should be viewed as an additional channel rather than as a replacement for traditional channels to consumers and business partners.

**The New Technology Adoption Lifecycle.**   The need to extend the radar will cause mainstream businesses to become more like pioneers and early adopters and over time may even reshape the classical technology adoption lifecycle which is shown in Figure 1-1. This adoption lifecycle was first developed during the technology diffusion studies of rural sociologists in the 1940s. The researchers were looking at the adoption rates of hybrid seed among Iowa farmers.

**Figure 1-1**   Traditional Technology Adoption Lifecycle.

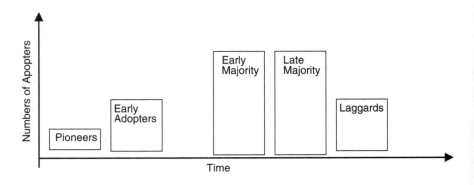

While the classical adoption lifecycle and its symmetric bell-shaped curve have held true and have been extensible to the software industry and business adoption of new technologies, this is no longer the case. The traditional curve took shape because communication channels were constrained and even the innovations themselves were not immediately widespread or accessible. Today, with the ability to communicate globally via the Internet and with the immediate accessibility of software innovations to those enterprises who are extending their radars, the diffusion and adoption of innovation can occur at a more rapid pace and via a skewed adoption curve. Figure 1-2 shows this new form of the technology adoption lifecycle.

When contrasted with the traditional technology adoption lifecycle, this new model illustrates how the chasm, or gap in the timing of further adoption, will be pushed back between the late majority and the laggards instead of between the early adopters and the early majority. While there will be a shift in the distribution of the adoption lifecycle in terms of the number of businesses adopting new technologies over different periods of time, there will still be a considerable time lag between the early adopters and the laggards. This is because certain innovations are not production ready upon initial discovery. It often takes time for the surrounding ecosystem of companies and products to create the mass market for the solution and to establish a baseline level of confidence and trust among the adopters.

**Figure 1-2**  New Technology Adoption Lifecycle.

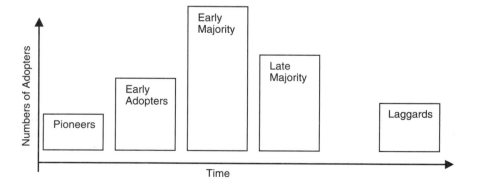

Adoption of emerging and disruptive technologies is a high-risk, high-reward proposition. Those who enter early and intelligently stand to gain considerable advantages but also expose themselves to an increased level of risk. Correct timing of market entry in terms of identification, prioritization, and adoption is critical. One of the benefits of extending the radar is that businesses will have more time to make these business-critical decisions since they can identify opportunity earlier. According to Charles Marinello, Director of Corporate Strategy at Texas Instruments, this is like having a more powerful missile detection system. Early warning of incoming threats can help provide more time to make decisions and to launch countermeasures in response.

The new technology adoption lifecycle is really a call to action for the business executive. You should plan to extend your radar, reshape your adoption curve in terms of how you identify, prioritize, and implement new technologies, and become a smart mover around new technologies and solutions. Chapter 8 presents some process steps for implementing this call to action to extend the radar.

# Enterprise Software Trends

## Return of the Major Players

On the supply side of the equation, within the independent software vendor arena, 2002 and beyond could well see the return to prominence of the major players—companies such as IBM, Microsoft, Oracle, SAP, and Sun Microsystems. Over the past three years, during the Internet boom, hundreds of startups came to power in a wide variety of market niches, stole some visibility and market share from these major players, and gained large market capitalization in the process. With the slowdown in business spending, many of these newer companies have been struggling for survival as revenues become scarce. Additionally, with stock levels and corresponding market capitalizations back to more normal levels, venture capitalists and private equity investors are becoming more selective in their investments, focusing much more effort on their existing portfolio investments, and are giving out lower valuations for those new companies they do decide to invest in.

The major players are now coming back to the table and are often leading in terms of innovation where previously in the Internet era they had occasionally fallen behind or had appeared to have fallen behind. The next wave of emerging technology innovation is being led by these major players who have the funds and resources to keep the industry advancing. Examples include Intel's peer-to-peer initiatives, Microsoft's .Net initiative, Sun's Open Network Environment (ONE) initiative, and Texas Instruments' work in the RFID area. Additionally, IBM's work in the Web services area, in conjunction with Microsoft and others, is helping to develop the core standards that serve as the foundation for Web services. These include standards such as Simple Object Access Protocol (SOAP), Universal Description, Discovery, and Integration (UDDI), and Web Services Description Language (WSDL). For those readers interested in learning more about these standards, Chapter 2 discusses the evolution of Web services from these first standards to the present and the creation of organizations such as the Web Services Interoperability Organization known as WS-I. An awareness of the major players and standards behind these changes in software industry direction can help businesses more fully exploit the potential of the technology. Web services is a megatrend that is reshaping the software industry and has great potential for reshaping many other industries as it evolves.

In addition to the re-emergence of the major players in terms of visibility and innovation, many other trends are shaping the software industry. Categories of software are becoming increasingly blurred and many appear to be converging. Even the concept of software is moving from a product-centric model to a service-centric model. Rather than a one-time event of purchase and installation, software is now becoming transformed into an ongoing service provided in a variety of pricing models for business customers to utilize. While application service providers suffered considerably over the past several years due to incomplete offerings, incorrectly priced services, and lack of acceptance of the outsourced model at the time, their fundamental business model—providing software services over networks such as the Internet for businesses to subscribe to—was accurate. The software-as-a-service movement (SaaS), which encompasses the application service provider model and several other models, means that software companies need to re-engineer themselves in terms of how they deliver value to businesses and how they monetize that value. The entire spectrum of software licensing needs to be redesigned to accommodate a variety of pricing models and new ways of packaging software elements into valuable business functions exposed as a service.

**Wireless Middleware Market.**   The wireless middleware software market serves as a good example of the return of the major players into niches that were previously filled by startups and specialty vendors. This market showed great promise a couple of years ago but now has too many vendors chasing too few opportunities among enterprise buyers. The wireless application middleware market is still here and is a large growth market, but too many vendors are aiming for dominance. At one time, there were over 100 vendors in the space including major public software companies, public wireless specialists, and private wireless specialists. These companies all aim to serve business by providing software infrastructure to support enterprise mobility via cell phones, personal digital assistants, and pagers. They aim to extend existing applications to any device over any wireless network and to move information and transactions to the point of business activity. They achieve this by transforming content from the typical desktop-sized displays to the much smaller formats and varied user interface designs found on wireless devices.

Today major companies such as IBM, Microsoft, Oracle, and Sybase are moving in to challenge public and privately held specialists such as 724 Solutions, Aether Systems, Air2Web, AvantGo, Brience, InfoWave, Research In Motion, and Wireless Knowledge. With technologies such as wireless and mobile enablement locked in early adopter status within the business due to tight IT budgets, many of the wireless specialists are hurting for revenues. The major software vendors can acquire these wireless specialists at extremely low valuations and effectively absorb their technology into their own portfolio. Companies that are not acquired are going out of business as they run out of cash reserves. Recent examples have included NetMorf and 2Roam. Both were companies with solid technology, management teams, and major customers, but due to market timing they unfortunately ran through their funds and were unable to raise subsequent rounds.

Enterprise buyers are also opting for safe bets by choosing solutions from vendors they know will be around in a year or more. Thus, in this example, technologies such as Mobile Information Server from Microsoft and WebSphere Everyplace Suite from IBM are seeing increased traction in terms of enterprise adoption in the wireless middleware arena. Those private and public wireless and mobile special-ists that are still in the game are pursuing a variety of options for strengthening their positions in the market. These options include glo-bal expansion to chase immediate revenues outside the United States; increased marketing activity to better position their offerings for enterprise return on investment as opposed to technical feature lists; increased focus on partnerships for channel sales through original equipment manufacturers (OEMs), resellers, and systems integrators; diversification of their core technologies into other related software categories; and deeper specialization within certain industry verticals.

This process of natural selection and evolution plays itself out in many categories of software. First movers come in and help develop the market, many go out of business or are acquired, and the fast fol-lowers come in to dominate the market once the demand has been ignited and the best practices and most effective value propositions have been determined.

## Convergence of Software Categories

Another trend occurring in the independent software vendor arena, in addition to the return of the major players, is the convergence of soft-ware categories. As the number of software vendors increased over the past couple of years, so did the number of categories of software. In addition to core categories such as enterprise resource planning, customer relationship management, and supply chain management, we now have software for partner relationship management, cus-tomer experience management, enterprise interaction management, and the list goes on.

With the slowdown in the economy, however, these categories have naturally started to converge at a faster rate as the larger compa-nies acquire these additional capabilities in order to extend their own core offerings for their customers. Supply chain management vendors have added collaborative commerce capabilities, application server vendors have added wireless middleware capabilities, and enterprise application integration vendors have added Web services capabilities. Additionally, the various players in the larger software industry value chain are taking on new roles: Systems integrators are adding man-aged service and business process outsourcing capabilities, indepen-dent software vendors are adding application service provider capabilities, and application service providers are adding systems integration capabilities.

This convergence of software categories is part of a process of natural evolution for the software industry. New categories spring up and the most promising become embedded into the core offerings of the strongest players as they build out their platform functionality. There is always a battle between those vendors aiming at platform dominance with a suite of software functionality for the enterprise and those aiming at being best-of-breed within a particular software application niche. Examples include IBM, Oracle, and Microsoft, who provide platform solutions and companies such as BEA and I2, who focus on being specialists in areas such as application servers and supply chain management.

## Software as a Service (SaaS)

One of the major trends in the software industry at the present time is the rise of software as a service, or SaaS. This approach to delivering and running software functionality over the network has been in practice for several years by many vendors such as Intuit and McAfee but is now becoming an option for most of the industry. The most well-known approach for software as a service is the application service provider or ASP. Other models, which may or may not differ slightly based upon the business models of the various companies, include application infrastructure provider (AIP), business service provider (BSP), and solutions service provider (SSP).

Software as a service represents a much larger trend in the software industry than the initial application service provider model that we have witnessed over the past several years. While ASPs have had their ups and downs in recent times, the longer term trend of software as a service stands to reshape the entire industry and to have a major impact on how the enterprise purchases and exploits software in the future.

The SaaS model delivers software functionality over the network, including Internet, intranet, local area network, and virtual private network delivery options, and helps software companies avoid the costly process of producing and distributing shrink-wrapped CD-ROMs to their customers. Additionally, software vendors can charge for their software services via ongoing subscription models instead of one-time license fees and annual support fees. This can help to smooth out revenue bumps associated with traditional one-time license fees and can open up a wider business audience for the vendor, thanks to the Internet delivery model. One of the challenges with shared services such as the application service provider model, however, is the determination of usage and pricing per customer. Today's electronic business applications are so complex that it is often hard to determine which customers are consuming the most amount of computing resources and to charge accordingly.

In certain cases, software vendors can take advantage of dynamic pricing and vary their pricing based upon enterprise or consumer demand at key points in time. Upgrades to software are also a lot easier for the software vendor to implement using software as a service: One change made on the network is cascaded to all users. Under the old paradigm, vendors had to ship upgrades and new product releases via shrink-wrapped software to each of their customers.

For the enterprise, one of the future benefits of this model includes the ability to combine multiple externally provided software services to form more complete solutions to its business problems. It can take the best-of-breed approach and combine elements of functionality from different vendors over the network—even down to the individual software component level. At least this is one of the goals of the software as a service movement.

One of the barriers to this end goal is that the software standards are still being defined. Making software components from different vendors talk to one another is still far from complete, but as we shall discover in our section on Web services, this is becoming far more possible today than it ever has been historically. We are on the verge of a monumental breakthrough in software interoperability where the holy grail of software interoperability and business process discovery is within sight. Software components written in different programming languages and running on different operating system platforms can now discover one another over the network and interoperate with one another, in effect, creating applications upon demand. Today, much of this integration is achieved with prearranged business partners. Tomorrow, the ad hoc assembly of business processes with new partners may also be within reach, assuming that trust issues and other fundamental business relationship factors can be resolved.

The SaaS movement is also subject to all the pros and cons of the outsourcing model. Typically, enterprise IT managers will outsource only certain aspects of application functionality in order to save time and lower cost for nonstrategic and noncore competency IT functions. They will outsource those elements that they feel comfortable placing in the hands of others, and, in so doing, will sacrifice some control and security over the content and applications. Typically, elements that may be outsourced include news and information feeds, data storage and backups, alerts and notifications, email functionality, desktop productivity enhancements, security upgrades, utilities, and, in the consumer market, entertainment and education. An example of software as a service in the consumer space is the relationship between Exent Technologies, an application infrastructure provider, and Bell Canada, a broadband service provider, for delivering subscription-based games-on-demand to Bell Canada's DSL subscribers.

**SaaS Value Chain.** The SaaS value chain is composed of hardware providers, software infrastructure providers, network service providers (NSPs), independent software vendors (ISVs), business process outsourcers (BPOs), and application service providers (ASPs). One or many of these providers may combine to provide the final software as a service solution to the end user. The end user can be a large enterprise, small or medium sized business, or consumer.

Figure 1-3 shows the software as a service value chain. Included within this value chain is the entire range of xSPs, including application infrastructure providers and application service providers.

**Figure 1-3** SaaS Value Chain.

# Key Emerging Technology Vendors

Table 1-2 shows some of the key emerging technology vendors in the various enterprise software categories that are the focus of this book. In most areas, the categories contain a mixture of public and private software companies ranging from those with multibillion-dollar market capitalizations such as IBM, Microsoft, Oracle, and Sun to small startups with 10s or 100s of millions of dollars in financing. These smaller vendors have a strong vision for where the industry is heading within their disciplines and have been gaining traction within the Fortune 500 enterprise. In addition to the major players, vendors such as Bowstreet and Grand Central Communications have been highly visible in the Web services arena. The same is true for Groove Networks in the peer services arena and KnowNow in the real-time enterprise arena. In business process management, Intalio and Fuego have been some of the early pioneers. Likewise, mFormation Technologies has been one of the early players in the wireless infrastructure management space. Many of these companies will be profiled later in the book within their respective chapters.

Table 1-2 shows a snapshot of some of the current players on the radar who are helping to move the industry forward within these software categories. The list is by no means all-inclusive but highlights some of the more visible players within each category.

**Table 1-2** Key Emerging Technology Vendors.

| Web Services | Peer Services and Collaboration | Real-Time Computing |
|---|---|---|
| - Asera | - Advanced Reality | - Bang Networks |
| - Avinon | - Autonomy | - CommerceEvents |
| - Bowstreet | - Cahoots | - DemandTec |
| - Cape Clear | - Endeavors Technology | - FineGround Networks |
| - Grand Central Communications | - Groove Networks | - IBM |
| - HP | - Intel | - KnowNow |
| - IBM | - Jabber | - Nonstop Solutions |
| - Kenamea | - McAfee AsaP | - OpenDesign |
| - Microsoft | - Microsoft "Hailstorm" | - PowerMarket |
| - Oracle | - NextPage | - Rapt |
| - Sun | - Oculus Technologies | - Savi Technology |
| | | - SeeBeyond |

Table 1-2    *(continued)*

| Web Services | Peer Services and Collaboration | Real-Time Computing |
|---|---|---|
| - Talaris<br>- UDICO | - OpenCola<br>- Sun Microsystems | - SeeCommerce<br>- Sun Microsystems<br>- Tibco<br>- Tilion<br>- Vigilance<br>- Vitria<br>- WebMethods<br>- WorldChain |

| Business Process Management | Mobile Business | Enterprise Security |
|---|---|---|
| - ATG<br>- Asera<br>- BEA<br>- BMC Software<br>- Bowstreet<br>- Commerce One<br>- CrossWorlds<br>- Epicentric<br>- Excelon<br>- Exigen<br>- Extricity<br>- FileNet<br>- Fuego<br>- HP<br>- IBM<br>- Intalio<br>- Intraspect<br>- Jamcracker<br>- Level 8<br>- Mercator<br>- PeopleSoft | **Wireless Infrastructure Management**<br>- mFormation Technologies Inc.<br>**Mobile Commerce**<br>- Nokia<br>**Embedded Systems**<br>- Intrinsyc<br>Location-Based Services<br>- Autodesk<br>- Cell-Loc<br>- SignalSoft<br>- Vindigo<br>- Webraska<br>**Telematics**<br>- Wingcast<br>**Electronic Tagging**<br>- Alien Technology<br>- Infineon<br>- Phillips Semiconductor | - Check Point Software<br>- Cisco Systems<br>- Computer Associates<br>- Network Associates<br>- Nokia<br>- RSA Security<br>- Symantec Corporation<br>- Tripwire<br>- Vigilinx<br>- Viisage<br>- Visionics |

Table 1-2    *(continued)*

| Business Process Management | Mobile Business | Enterprise Security |
|---|---|---|
| - Rational | - STMicroelectronics | |
| - SAP | - Texas Instruments | |
| - SeeBeyond | | |
| - SilverStream | | |
| - Sterling Commerce | | |
| - Sun Microsystems | | |
| - Sybase | | |
| - Systar | | |
| - Taviz | | |
| - Tibco Software | | |
| - Vignette | | |
| - Vitria | | |
| - webMethods | | |
| - Zaplet | | |

# Key Applications

It is important to explore some of the fundamentals and business benefits behind the main technology categories and disciplines under investigation: Web services, peer services, real-time computing, business process management, mobile business, and enterprise security. These categories are all infrastructure areas that cut across multiple industries and multiple enterprise user constituencies; each can be applied to specific business processes and application areas for employees, customers, and partners. While enterprise security is not necessarily an emerging technology, it is included here since it is an increasingly important subject for businesses as they seek not only to create new forms of competitive advantage, but also to protect the competitive advantage and assets that they already have in place. As we shall see in the following section, these software categories and disciplines together represent a refocus on infrastructure that will create a new generation of enterprise software applications and new opportunities for enhancing enterprise value.

The business benefits of this next class of applications are perhaps stronger than the previous wave of applications that we saw in the original e-business era of the late 1990s. While e-business helped to connect humans to information and applications, the next evolution of software and the Internet will help to connect applications and business processes together, both intraenterprise and interenterprise. E-business will move from a mostly human-to-machine interaction to an entirely new universe of machine-to-machine and object-to-object interactions, setting the stage for ubiquitous computing. Web services, peer services, real-time computing, business process management, and mobile business will all serve as enablers for this next generation of business applications and for the ubiquitous computing vision to become a reality.

## Refocus on Infrastructure

The software industry tends to move in waves, or cycles, as it evolves and matures. While the mid- to late 1990s were focused on packaged applications for functional areas such as enterprise resource planning, customer relationship management, and supply chain management, the next wave for the industry is a refocus on infrastructure: the horizontal or platform software capabilities that serve as enablers for all of these functional application areas.

This infrastructure software can be considered the building blocks, or behind-the-scenes components, that help to make everything run smoothly and transparently. To use a race car analogy, the infrastructure comprises all the components and processes that help to operate the car and relay vital information back to the pits, which are, for the most part, unseen by the driver. The driver, of course, monitors this infrastructure via communications with the pits and via his own dashboard. Along with a skilled driver, this infrastructure can make the difference between winning and losing.

When the Internet became a new infrastructure platform for the deployment of enterprise software applications, pushing many client/server applications into the history books, software vendors rushed in to develop and sell vertical software applications for specific industries and functional areas. The basic Internet infrastructure in terms of protocols and standards was fairly unsophisticated at the time, and still is, but software companies managed to enhance the session-less request/response paradigm of the Internet and offer compelling applications for business users that maintained the state of the users' session. This was achieved  by using client- and server-side scripts and software components such as Java applets and ActiveX controls. As we all know, the Internet and the Web were originally designed for simple email, document exchange, and the display of static content, not for sophisticated and dynamic business applications that require access to back-end systems and databases.

Despite the limitations of the earlier Internet protocols and standards, these new vendor applications retained an acceptable level of user experience while using the compelling benefits of the Internet in terms of ease of development and deployment. Client/server applications had historically been very difficult to distribute to end users due to their "thick-client" nature, i.e., software and drivers had to be installed on each individual PC or laptop client in order to run the applications. In the client/server days, application releases, bug fixes, and upgrades were notoriously difficult and time consuming.

## Into the Internet II Era

Now that the software industry has built out the functional application side for the enterprise, it is turning its attention back to the infrastructure layer and looking for ways to essentially build an Internet II—a new, more intelligent layer of infrastructure software between applications and the network that can significantly enhance business value.

There is, in fact, an Internet2 consortium made up of "over 190 universities working in partnership with industry and government to develop and deploy advanced network applications and technologies, accelerating the creation of tomorrow's Internet." The consortium works closely with the National Science Foundation (NSF) and other U.S. Federal Government research agencies. The Internet2 community is working on advances in applications, middleware, and networks and plans to offer 10-gigabit capacity by 2003.

The term Internet II is used loosely here, however, and is unrelated to the Internet2 consortium. The former term merely seeks to illustrate how the vendors are aiming to build enhanced capabilities on top of the basic infrastructure of the Internet and in so doing are opening up new possibilities for the enterprise decision-maker to extract business value. Extensible Markup Language or XML, as you might expect, is also playing a key role as an enabling technology for these solutions. Basically, the standards are maturing and becoming more open and interoperable, allowing more powerful business applications to be constructed on top of the underlying infrastructure.

Web services and peer services are two perfect examples. Both represent innovations that are reshaping the realm of possibilities for the business to create and deploy superior Internet-centric applications on both a technical level and a business level. We'll continue by looking at these two application areas and then move on to other exciting and overlapping areas, including real-time computing and business process management.

## Web Services

Web services are perhaps one of the most exciting new areas within the emerging technology landscape. They truly have the potential to reshape entire industries and are closely connected with the SaaS movement.

Web services allow enterprises to communicate with one another in a business-to-business scenario by exposing their services programmatically over the Internet. Other enterprises may then search for, discover, and integrate with these services in an automated machine-to-machine manner. Ultimately, Web services presents the "holy grail" for business-to-business integration: business process discovery among business partners. Instead of publishing static content on the Internet, or dynamic, database-driven content for end users to interact with, companies are now able to publish entire transactional business processes via software. These business processes can be executed in a fully automated manner via the systems of customers and business partners without requiring those customers or business partners to know about the services ahead of time.

Web services can also be applied inside the corporate firewall in order to streamline enterprise application integration initiatives or even for enterprise portal development initiatives. The current evolution of Web services is expected to progress from internal application integration, to business-to-business integration with prearranged business partners, and finally to true business-to-business integration with dynamically discovered business partners. The latter will most likely gain adoption only in niche, commoditized areas where business trust issues related to dealing with unknown companies do not present a substantial business risk.

Electronic data interchange, or EDI, as a technique for integration between companies has been around since the mid-70s, but Web services promise to make enterprise application integration far more flexible and interoperable. They can help applications talk to one another independent of programming language or operating system by making the communication more loosely coupled and standardized. Additionally, a host of new business models can be created by combining Web services from a variety of business partners into powerful new offerings.

The research firm IDC expects the global market for Web services to triple from $22 billion in 2000 to $69 billion in 2005. All major software companies, including IBM (WebSphere), Microsoft (.Net), Oracle (Web Services Framework) and Sun (ONE), have announced strategies and platforms to support this emerging technology. In fact, Microsoft has already made an initial $5 billion investment on .Net, their Web services initiative. Additional new entrants in the Web services arena include companies such as Asera, Avinon, Bowstreet, Cape Clear, Grand Central Communications, Kenamea, Talaris, and UDICO. WS-I, announced in early 2002, was another milestone for the overall movement and will help ensure that Web services from different vendors stand the best chances for interoperability. The Web services value chain includes infrastructure services, platform services, directory services, aggregation and portal services, and, finally, business and consumer services. The value chain is being assembled and driven by the software industry, but the benefits for business users are compelling.

The business benefits of Web services include cost reduction via reduced IT expenses for enterprise application integration software and services and increased revenue opportunities via software as a service providing automated links with business partners for transaction fees and referral fees. Web services also help the enterprise move closer to the concept of the virtual enterprise by allowing core business functions to be published as Web services and other noncore business functions to be outsourced and subscribed to as Web services. As businesses start to unbundle their business functions and digitize them into software, Web services provide them with a new mechanism for exposing these services in an interoperable and accessible manner. For example, a company moving to an IT shared services model can use Web services to expose application functionality for other operating companies to use within the same organization. It can then assess charge-backs for use of these services.

An example of a company already gaining an advantage from Web services is Dollar Rent-A-Car. The company used Web services technology from Microsoft to integrate its online booking system with the Southwest Airlines Web site. The company expects to save hundreds of thousands of dollars by routing bookings through automated airline sites versus through travel agent networks. In this scenario, Web services technology is automating business-to-business transactions and disintermediating traditional aggregators of services. The ability to more easily connect systems between business partners has reduced the need for third parties to serve as brokers for the transactions. As another example of Web services, DuPont Performance Coatings used Web services technology from Bowstreet to create a customer portal for distributors and body shops in the automotive industry. The solution yielded increased business rule flexibility, end-user management, and mass customization of the portal when compared to more traditional development environments for constructing Web portals.

## Peer Services

The concept of peer-to-peer computing was popularized by companies such as Napster in the consumer space with their controversial file-sharing community for the exchange of media files. The peer-to-peer concept has actually been around for decades and was used extensively in the early days of corporate networking in local area network products such as Microsoft Windows for Workgroups, Novell Personal NetWare, and IBM peer-to-peer Systems Network Architecture (SNA) networks.

Peer-to-peer computing is now becoming an increasingly important technology within the business community. Peer-to-peer basically leverages computers on the network "edge" (desktops) instead of centralized servers for performing various content, collaborative, and resource-sharing functions between client, or peer, computers on the network.

One of the major players in this field is Groove Networks, a company whose product lets groups create workspaces to share files, use message boards, mark up virtual whiteboards, engage in instant-messaging, have voice chat sessions, and much more. Groove Networks was founded in 1997 by Ray Ozzie, one of the original creators of Lotus Notes in the mid-1980s. Peer-to-peer computing goes beyond person-to-person collaboration for knowledge management purposes and also includes distributed content management and distributed computing cycles. Examples of its application for distributed computing cycles include the Intel Philanthropic Peer-to-Peer Program which focuses on a variety of scientific research efforts, including cancer research, and the SETI@home program which focuses on processing data from the radio telescope in Arecibo, Puerto Rico. SETI, or the Search for Extraterrestrial Intelligence, is a scientific program seeking to detect signs of intelligent life outside the planet Earth.

The analysts anticipate a strong market for peer-to-peer technologies within the business community due to the solid business benefits they enable. The Aberdeen Group and AMR Research expect corporate spending on collaboration software to triple from $10.6 billion in 2001 to $33.2 billion by 2004. The analyst firm IDC estimates that Fortune 500 corporations will lose $31.5 billion by 2003 due to rework and the inability to find information. Likewise, Meta Group states that workers spend approximately 25 to 35 percent of their time searching for the information they need, rather than working on strategic projects and business opportunities. Peer-to-peer computing has the potential to address many of these pain points within the business by opening up all computing resources for the searching and sharing of business information and for richer forms of collaboration.

Current initiatives in the world of peer-to-peer computing include Intel's Peer-to-Peer Working Group and Peer-to-Peer Trusted Library, and Sun's Project Juxtapose (JXTA). These initiatives aim to help build standards, protocols, and best practices so that corporate developers can focus on business applications for peer-to-peer technologies rather than building the infrastructure themselves. Some of the issues which these initiatives are currently addressing include the increased requirements for security, management, and interoperability that peer-to-peer computing requires, as opposed to the standard client/server model. Business users are understandably nervous about opening up their personal computers for resource sharing and for others to search and access. Some of the vendors and products in the peer-to-peer space include Groove Networks, NextPage, OpenCola, Advanced Reality, Microsoft Messenger, Yahoo Messenger and Groups, and Intranets.com.

One of the business benefits of peer services is improved employee productivity through the use of peer-to-peer collaborative platforms. These platforms allow groups to conduct business processes in a far richer collaborative environment than the simple email, phone, and fax interactions typical today when collaborating with business partners and customers. According to Groove, the technology helps people in different companies or different divisions reduce their "cost of connection" in collaborating with one another and performing their work. Business processes that can be enhanced and extended through the use of peer-to-peer collaborative platforms include purchasing, inventory control, distribution, exchanges and auctions, channel and partner relationship management, and customer care and support. Additional benefits of peer-to-peer computing include the ability to better utilize computing cycles on workstations across the business and the ability to better search and share content residing on knowledge worker desktops. Intel's NetBatch initiative, started in 1990, enabled the company to save hundreds of millions of dollars by using existing workstations on a global basis for large processing tasks related to their Engineering Design Application (EDA) environment and other initiatives.

## Real-Time Computing

Real-time computing aims to enhance enterprise value by speeding business processes. In this manner, the enterprise can speed operations and sense and react to changes in its internal and external environment more quickly than its competitors, thus decreasing cycle times, reducing costs, and improving productivity.

There are many areas within the business that can benefit from real-time computing. These include interactions with employees, customers, and partners. One of the challenges for the business is to determine which business processes are capable of this change, which will actually benefit from this change, and which will yield the most favorable return on investment for real-time enablement. To determine this return, the business should generally look at the amount of cost takeout that can be achieved via real-time enablement and understand the amount of process change that needs to occur and the associated costs in implementing this change. Some business processes have natural frequencies that cannot be streamlined, while others are ripe for optimization. An area that has gained considerable attention recently is the reporting of financial results to the investment community. This is an area that can be improved considerably and may help to take some of the surprises out of financial reporting for both management and investors if it is moved to a more frequent timeframe. Homeland security is obviously another key area where real-time intelligence and information dissemination are critical.

The real-time arena has a natural overlap with mobile business technology since, for business processes to move closer to real-time scenarios, information and transactions need to be able to move from source to destination regardless of location. Human approval processes may also be a part of a larger business process that is being streamlined, so real-time computing requires mobile business techniques in order to reach key employees at any time and any place.

Software vendors in the real-time computing arena include KnowNow, Bang Networks, FineGround Networks, and OpenDesign. Many vendors in this space position their technology as an alternative to costly enterprise application integration (EAI) initiatives and state that real-time computing helps to move EAI functionality to the network. The technology usually aims to implement a two-way communication mechanism between various applications and uses Internet protocols such as the Hypertext Transfer Protocol, the communication protocol between browsers and Web servers, as the transport vehicle for the communication to take place. Real-time computing enables powerful and flexible methods for controlling data flow, aggregation, and analysis, acting in some ways like a hardware router in moving information to the appropriate systems.

One of the additional benefits of real-time computing is that it forces the business to focus on key performance indicators and key metrics and can help employees focus on the work activities that matter the most. When business processes are energized in this way, real-time computing can also help expose and correct weaknesses in data quality and process bottlenecks, or simply bad processes, that were less apparent under the former processes and procedures.

## Business Process Management

Business process management, or BPM, is affecting enterprise application deployments on a number of levels. As an evolution of traditional enterprise application integration, it is helping to force a top-down view of the world from a business perspective rather than a bottom-up view from an IT perspective in order to solve business problems. Traditionally, a business requirement has been implemented via software by connecting databases together or by connecting applications together. Business process management views the world from a process orchestration perspective where business processes need to be created, executed, and managed. Business process management also allows business processes to be rapidly redesigned in order to meet changing business requirements. Business processes are allowed to span applications, devices, and people as discrete nodes within the overall set of process steps.

Software vendors in the business process management space include companies such as Fuego, Intalio, and Systar which focus exclusively on business services orchestration, business process management, and business process performance management, respectively. These companies target industry verticals such as telecommunications, energy, and financial services in functional areas such as customer relationship management, enterprise resource planning, and supply chain management. Additionally, most integration middleware vendors such as BEA, Vitria, and webMethods are beginning to support BPM functionality as a core product feature.

The business benefits for business process management include increased flexibility, reduction of complexity, decreased cost of ownership, and faster return on investment. One of the advantages of the process view ingrained into the BPM paradigm is that it helps the enterprise take a holistic view of its business transactions. It crosses internal and external boundaries in terms of data, applications, and people. It also helps to cross the conceptual boundaries between wired and wireless transactions which are really just different modes of connection to the network. Finally, BPM helps to focus the enterprise and IT operations on business processes and metrics and not IT metrics. In many enterprise scenarios, business metrics can fail even when IT metrics are satisfactory. For example, server uptime is independent of whether or not a key business customer has placed an expected order or whether or not a financial transaction has been settled in time in order to avoid financial penalties.

Business process management is an important set of functionality that can help to speed integration of applications and empower end users to play a more vital role in the overall modeling and orchestration of their business processes.

## Mobile Business

Mobile business is another area that cuts across numerous industry verticals and numerous functional and horizontal areas; it can be applied to functional application areas such as customer relationship management and field force automation, and also to horizontal application areas such as corporate email, personal information management, executive dashboards for the aggregation of business-critical information, and business intelligence applications.

Mobile business represents an opportunity to move information and transactions to the point of business activity and to remove former process bottlenecks for mobile employees. It represents a way to increase the reach and value of technology within one's business by extending it to any employee, any customer, and any partner, anywhere and any time. The opportunity exists both to refine existing processes and to create entirely new ones.

Mobile employees now have the ability to leverage technology just as if they were in the office. Improvements in devices, applications, networks, and standards over the past few years have made this far more practical than it was when first introduced. The drivers for adoption are finally starting to outweigh the barriers. For example, major vendors such as IBM, Microsoft, Oracle, and Sybase are all playing a larger role and taking a larger interest in mobile business than they had previously. These vendors all have mature, proven offerings for enterprise mobility. Additionally, the wireless carriers are rolling out "2.5G" and "3G Lite" networks such as General Packet Radio Service (GPRS) in the United States that enable higher bandwidths for wireless data. Devices are making strong strides forward in terms of usability and features. Microsoft's Pocket PC 2002 is a notable example of one of the latest operating systems. Standards such as Extensible HTML (XHTML), Binary Runtime Environment for Wireless (BREW), Java 2 Platform Micro Edition (J2ME), and Wireless Application Protocol (WAP) 2.0 are all having an impact as well. They are helping to make mobile business easier for both developers and end users by enriching the functionality available on mobile devices.

Mobile business technology helps to extend the corporation out to its edges in areas such as sales force automation, field force automation, and enterprise operations. Benefits can include improved data accuracy, reduced costs, increased productivity, increased revenues, and improved customer service. Beyond being an additional channel for communications, mobile business enables the enterprise to think about the powerful combination of business process, e-business, and wireless communications. Instead of being at the intersection of e-business and wireless communications, it often helps to think of mobile business as being a superset of e-business and wireless that also includes business process.

In *Business Agility*, I took an in-depth look at mobile business and how it can be applied for competitive advantage within the enterprise. In *Business Innovation and Disruptive Technology*, we'll extend the radar further and look at upcoming areas within the field of mobile business, including mobile commerce, location-based services, telematics, and electronic tagging. These are all interesting subcategories within mobile business that open up new opportunities for mobility beyond simple employee applications. Embedded computing and electronic tagging are especially interesting because they extend wireless and mobile technologies not just to humans but also to a wide range of objects such as consumer and industrial products. These products can gain intelligence via electronic product codes, which are a potential replacement for universal product code (UPC) barcodes, and via RFID tags with two-way communication capabilities.

## Enterprise Security

Enterprise security is an area that is perhaps the most fundamental and yet the most critical of all the technologies and disciplines for the business to have squarely in place in order to execute on its business strategy. Without solid enterprise security processes and procedures, none of the other technologies can be reliably applied for business advantage. Security is no longer just a luxury. Today it is a business imperative. Business disruption can be not only an inconvenience for business users and their customers and partners, it can also cost millions of dollars in lost revenues or lost market capitalization. But the business cost of inadequate security does not stop at simply inconvenience and loss of revenues or market valuation. It can even force a business out of existence. One of the earliest examples of this was the case in early 2002 for British Internet service provider CloudNine Communications, which was the victim of a distributed denial-of-service (DDOS) attack that forced the company to close operations and to eventually transfer over 2,500 customers to a rival organization. While emerging technologies can help a company to gain competitive advantage and market share, lack of security can have the opposite effect, causing profitable companies to lose market share or even their entire business within hours or days of an attack.

Fortunately, the security arms race in terms of attacks and prevention measures is not all one-sided. As hackers exploit vulnerabilities, so software companies and enterprise security specialists continue to close the gaps and find new solutions and approaches to secure enterprise operations and data. One of the challenges facing enterprise security is that it is often very difficult to know when enterprise networks and applications have been attacked or are in the process of being attacked. Because of this, security measures within emerging solutions are becoming increasingly proactive. Instead of simply responding once a business system has been compromised, businesses are moving toward real-time proactive monitoring of their operations and employing intrusion detection tools that can help to spot illegal or unusual activity on the network. With these tools in place, activities that would have gone hitherto unnoticed are detected while they are in progress and can either be instantly blocked or have their actions immediately reported to enterprise security administrators or law enforcement for rapid response.

Some of the categories of software and services in the enterprise security arena include biometrics, intrusion detection, encryption, vulnerability assessment, managed security services, and general security management. Security management typically includes functions for what is termed "3A": administration, authorization, and authentication. The analyst firm IDC estimates that the total IT security market will grow from over $14 billion in 2000 to $46 billion by 2005. This market estimate includes security software, hardware, and services. It expects the security software market alone to reach over $14 billion by 2005 and be comprised of security "3As," firewalls, antiviral software, and encryption technologies. Companies in the security hardware, software, and services arena include well-established vendors such as Computer Associates, Cisco Systems, Symantec Corporation, Network Associates, Check Point Software, Nokia, and RSA Security, together with newcomers such as Tripwire, Vigilinx, Viisage, and Visionics.

Business benefits in deploying the latest advances in security technologies include the cost avoidance of greater disruptions without such technologies, together with increases in productivity of employees due to coordinated approaches for administration, authorization, and authentication. As the number of applications and modes of access to the network increases within the business, the importance of single sign-on technologies and efficient management of security profiles cannot be underestimated. An additional business benefit related to security is compliance. In many industries such as health care and financial services, businesses face government regulations which require consumer privacy protection. An example is the Health Insurance Portability and Accountability Act (HIPAA) within the health care industry where techniques such as encryption can help protect stored or transmitted data from unauthorized viewing or alteration.

# Summary

This new wave of technology innovation will cause massive changes in the way that business can be conducted, opening up the business world to the world of ubiquitous computing. The next phase of the software and Internet evolution will start to merge bits with atoms—a concept promoted by the M.I.T. Auto-ID Center, which focuses its research on electronic tagging of physical objects. The physical world and the virtual world will become increasingly connected as computing devices and physical objects of all kinds gain intelligence and the ability to communicate with the network via wired and wireless technologies and intelligent identification techniques such as electronic product codes and RFID systems. Web services and peer services will allow objects and applications increasingly to communicate with one another in an interoperable manner. Real-time computing will create business benefits from improved efficiencies and reduced cycle times. Mobile business will keep people connected to the network and will allow devices to be tracked and monitored. Business process management will enable nontechnical end users to manage their business processes across multiple organizations and do so in a language they can understand. Enterprise security will help strengthen business resiliency and will serve as an enabler for these new forms of interaction to occur in a safe, trusted environment.

In the following chapters, we take a detailed look at each of these emerging and disruptive technology categories. Within each chapter we will explore the market, the technology, and industry scenarios and benefits related to each emerging technology. The market section will cover the drivers for adoption; the recent history in terms of standards, applications, and vendors; the value chain that is being assembled in order to deliver end-to-end business solutions within this category; and profiles of some of the major vendors in the space. The technology section will briefly cover some of the concepts and fundamentals that are important for executives to understand when assessing these technologies for their business. Finally, the industry scenarios section will describe typical industry situations where these technologies can be applied and the business benefits that can be realized.

# Extending the Radar Lessons

>> Enterprise business trends include increased economic uncertainty, focus on productivity and cost takeout, focus on security and resiliency, and the business management of information technology.

>> Within enterprise IT departments, the need to extend the radar and look for new forms of competitive advantage will cause mainstream enterprises to become more like pioneers and early adopters of emerging technology. Over time, this effect may even reshape the classical technology adoption lifecycle.

>> Enterprise software trends include the movement to SaaS, the return of the major players, a re-emphasis on infrastructure services, and the convergence of software categories.

>> Emerging and disruptive technologies include Web services, peer services, real-time computing, business process management, mobile business, and enterprise security. Security is a key defensive measure to support the baseline operation and resiliency of the business as it pursues these new business enablers.

>>   These emerging technologies will cause massive changes in the way that business can be conducted, opening up the business world to the world of ubiquitous computing where "bits and atoms are merged."

>>   The physical world and the virtual world will become increasingly connected as computing devices and physical objects of all kinds gain intelligence and the ability to communicate with one another.

# Chapter

# 2

# Web Services

*"As a result of the changes in how businesses and consumers use the Web, the industry is converging on a new computing model that enables a standard way of building applications and processes to connect and exchange information over the Web."*

—Bill Gates, Microsoft

W eb services are currently the most promising "next new thing" in the software industry and are starting to gain some visibility in the business world as success stories from the pioneers and early adopters become known. Web services promise to usher in a new evolution of computing with impacts for both business and technology strategies. The technology enables business services, including applications, information, and tasks, to be exposed as software services running on the network. These network-resident services can be published and subscribed to by other such services running over standard Internet protocols and open standards. The potential business benefits of Web services include the opportunity to enter new markets via new service offerings, increased business agility, improved competitive advantage, and migration toward the virtual enterprise. Increased business agility is enabled because Web services enable software components to more easily talk to one another across disparate operating systems and programming languages. Migration toward the virtual enterprise is enabled since businesses now have a powerful and standardized mechanism by which to unbundle and expose their business functionality and business processes as software.

Over the past two years, Web services have captured the imagination of the broader software community, venture capitalists, analysts and media, and the general business community. This buzz of activity has surrounded the continued development of standards, the launch of new Web services platforms and development environments, and the activities of both the "big five" vendors—namely Hewlett-Packard, IBM, Microsoft, Oracle, and Sun—and a number of new entrants such as Bowstreet, Cape Clear, and Grand Central Communications. Another landmark event was the announcement of the Web Services Interoperability Organization (WS-I) in early 2002. The organization is chartered to work "across a number of standards organizations to respond to customer needs by providing guidance, best practices, and resources for developing Web services solutions." Thus far, with a few notable exceptions, the mainstream business community has been content to observe, learn, and perform some initial, internal proof of concepts and low-risk deployments. One of the challenges for the business executive has been to determine what exactly Web services are all about and how, when, and where they should be applied within the corporation.

With so much activity going on in the Web services arena in terms of standards, applications, business models, and new entrants, it is worth taking a look back to see how this area of the industry has evolved, almost under the radar in some cases, and is building a new value chain among industry participants. By understanding this new value chain, the business decision maker will be able to understand the angle from which various software vendors are attacking the space and where they fit in terms of providing business solutions. It will also help to reveal some of the current gaps and white spaces in the current form of the technology which may impact the timing of business adoption.

# Market

It will be helpful to take a high-level overview of the Web services timeline and put the various standards initiatives and vendor product announcements into some form of historical perspective. The Web services arena is obviously a still-emerging area, in the pioneer and early adopter stage for business decision makers, that is continuing to unfold. A look back over the past couple of years can help to illustrate where the industry has come from, where it is today, and where it is heading. From this brief historical perspective, we can better understand how the new value chain is being assembled and how each of the major players and new entrants fits into it.

## Web Services Evolution

The evolution to Web services from other computing paradigms, integration approaches, and standards such as electronic data interchange, enterprise application integration, distributed object computing, and Internet protocols has been frequently told. Instead, we'll start our story with a discussion of the initial drivers for Web services and then look at more recent history focusing on actual Web services standards and applications.

## Drivers for Adoption

The driving force for the enterprise IT department to consider Web services has been the increasing complexity of the IT environment, the decrease in human and capital resources available per initiative, and the increasing focus on integration both within and outside the corporate firewall. IT departments have sought less costly approaches for application integration due to the heavy price tag typically associated with these efforts. Typical integration efforts attempting to link disparate computer systems take months or years, require a vast number of developers, and incur large costs due to the software licenses required and the time spent on integration and testing. Additionally, even when these integration initiatives have been completed, the business processes may have changed and the technical integration solutions can often be too inflexible to support these changes in business requirements.

On the business side, the enterprise has provided other drivers for Web services adoption, which include the search for new sources of revenue, new forms of business agility, competitive advantage, and the ongoing migration towards the virtual enterprise. The Internet and the World Wide Web helped the business take its first steps in migrating to a virtual enterprise, exposing business services as software, but the linkages were content-based rather than application-based. The Web enabled the virtualization of content, but linkages at the business application level were still hard to implement. Web services promise to extend the Internet functionality to support the virtual enterprise at both the content level and the application level, enabling virtual business processes to occur seamlessly and dynamically across organizational boundaries.

On the supply side of the equation within the software industry, the movement toward network-centric computing with open standards and Internet-oriented applications has served as an enabler for Web services to mature and to provide a new solution for these application integration challenges. Other drivers for Web services have included the software as a service movement within the software industry and its search for new pricing models which can yield ongoing subscription revenues instead of one-time license fees. In this way, drivers for the adoption of Web services have come from both the demand side of the equation and the supply side of the equation; both groups stand to extract value as Web services mature. Figure 2-1 illustrates some of these key drivers for the adoption of Web services.

## Recent History

The year 2000 and beyond are important periods in the evolution of Web services. In 2000, the three cornerstone standards behind Web services were first proposed: SOAP, UDDI, and WSDL.

**Figure 2-1**  Drivers for Adoption of Web Services.

**Enterprise (Demand Side)**                          **Software Industry (Supply Side)**

**IT Forces**
Increasing complexity of IT environment
Decrease in human and capital resources
Increased focus on integration

**Industry Forces**
Software as a service
New pricing models
Network-centric computing
Open standards
Internet protocols

**Web services**

**Business Forces**
Cost reduction for integration
New sources of revenue
Competitive advantage
Business agility
Virtual enterprise

**Emerging Standards**
XML
SOAP
UDDI
WSDL
.NET
J2EE

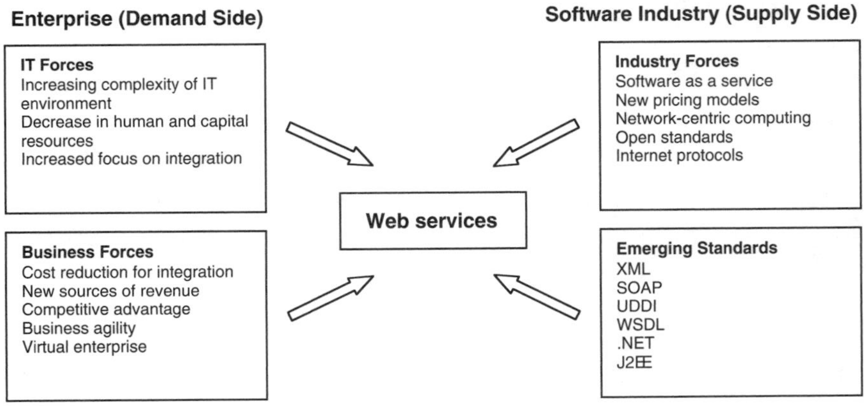

SOAP was first released by Microsoft in September 1999. It basically lets one application invoke a remote procedure call on another application and provides a way to pass objects embedded in XML messages between applications. SOAP can be considered the mechanism by which software components, distributed across a network such as the Internet, are able to talk with one another in a loosely coupled manner. This "loose coupling" allows software components, written in different programming languages and running on different operating systems, to interact over a variety of network protocols and to hide the specifics of their internal applications and systems. Previous forms of software component interaction, such as the Common Object Request Broker Architecture (CORBA) from the Object Management Group (OMG) and the Distributed Component Object Model (DCOM) from Microsoft, were tightly coupled and required extensive knowledge of the structure of their interaction and the same, or compatible, systems on both sides.

The major landmark for the SOAP standard was the release of version 1.1 in May 2000 with involvement from IBM and Microsoft. Version 1.1 supported a larger number of transport protocols for carrying SOAP documents than the initial version 1.0, which relied purely on Hypertext Transfer Protocol (HTTP), the communications protocol for Web servers on the Internet. Due to its early start, SOAP is currently one of the more robust, usable standards of the three major Web services standards. Support for SOAP interactions is incorporated into many hundreds of software vendors' products.

The next Web services initiative and standard to gain attention was UDDI. This cross-industry initiative was initially introduced by Ariba, IBM, and Microsoft in mid-2000. UDDI enables a business to describe its business and its services, discover other businesses that offer desired services, and integrate with these other businesses. The public beta UDDI Business Registry went live in November 2000.

The third Web services standard, WSDL, was released in October 2000. It was introduced by the same three companies who helped create the UDDI initiative: Ariba, IBM, and Microsoft. WSDL incorporated some earlier standards from IBM and Microsoft and provided a way for companies to describe and discover Web services located in UDDI registries.

In 2001, there was a flurry of activity in the Web services arena in terms of continued standards enhancements and the major vendors bringing Web services technology to market in the form of development tools, application servers, and public consumer-oriented Web services. October 2001 saw the announcement of the ONE initiative. This was Sun's "vision, architecture, platform, and expertise for building and deploying Services on Demand." Early 2002 saw the launch of Microsoft's Visual Studio.NET for Web services-based Internet application development, and the announcement of the WS-I.

---

# Microsoft .NET My Services

Microsoft's .NET My Services has consumer services exposed on the Internet for users to manage their profile, contacts, location, alerts, presence, inbox, calendar, documents, application settings, favorite Web sites, wallet, device, services, lists, and categories. It serves as a network-centric service and information repository for frequent consumer tasks and activities. Information can be shared across a variety of "endpoints" such as applications, devices, and services regardless of the technical platform of that endpoint in terms of operating system, object model, programming language, or network provider. Additionally, developers can leverage these Web services when building their own higher level Web services applications that need to incorporate this type of functionality. They can also create and expose their own .Net My Services-compatible services.

The business problem that all this solves is that it helps to create one place for user information to be stored and managed and to make it accessible for all other applications, devices, and individuals to access based upon their access privileges. It helps to eliminate all the silos of functionality and data across the Internet. The major issue involved in these types of consumer-oriented services is a trust issue about the privacy of information and which companies or organizations should be able to serve as the repository.

---

Table 2-1 shows the Web services timeline for the past couple of years, highlighting events in the standards, development tools, and platforms arena. The number of acronyms in this Web services evolution may seem daunting, but the main take-away for the business reader is that with standards and tools in place, and with major vendors driving the industry forwards, the groundwork has been set for true business value to be extracted from Web services as a critical enabling technology.

**Table 2-1**    Web Services Timeline: Standards, Development Tools, and Platforms.

| Date | Event | Companies |
|------|-------|-----------|
| September 1999 | SOAP v1.0 | Microsoft |
| May 2000 | SOAP v1.1 | IBM, Microsoft |
| July 2000 | .NET | Microsoft |
| Mid-2000 | UDDI | Ariba, IBM, Microsoft |
| October 2000 | WSDL | Ariba, IBM, Microsoft |
| November 2000 | Beta UDDI Business Registry Live | UDDI.org |
| December 2000 | Oracle 9i Dynamic Services and Dev. Kit | Oracle |
| March 2001 | WebSphere Technology for Developers | IBM |
| March 2001 | "HailStorm" | Microsoft |
| May 2001 | UDDI Registries Live | UDDI.org |
| June 2001 | UDDI v2 | UDDI.org |
| June 2001 | WebSphere Application Server v4 | IBM |
| June 2001 | Oracle 9i Application Server | Oracle |
| October 2001 | Sun Open Net Environment (ONE) | Sun |
| October 2001 | Preview .NET Alerts | Microsoft |
| October 2001 | Global XML Web Services Architecture | Microsoft |
| October 2001 | WS-Inspection | IBM and Microsoft |
| December 2001 | Oracle 9i Jdeveloper | Oracle |
| December 2001 | Orbix E2A Web Services Platform | Iona |
| February 2002 | Visual Studio .NET | Microsoft |
| February 2002 | Web Services Interoperability Organization (WS-I) | BEA, HP, IBM, Intel, Microsoft, Oracle, SAP, and others |

## Web Services Value Chain

These standards and product activities, as well as many other activities, during the past couple of years, have helped to rally the software industry around Web services and to encourage existing software players, as well as new entrants, to think about how Web services will impact their products in the future. Many vendors have incorporated support into their products and some have refocused their solutions to aim squarely at the space.

A high-level value chain for Web services is shown in Figure 2-2. The major sections of the value chain are comprised of infrastructure services, platform services, registry services, aggregation and portal services, and business services. This is somewhat similar to the traditional e-business value chain with a few exceptions such as registry services. The main difference is that all of these functions within the value chain are now moved to the network and exposed as a service using open Web services standards and common Internet protocols. For example, within infrastructure management, functions such as asset and configuration management are exposed as services for IT staff to access over the Internet with "software-as-a-service" pricing models instead of typical one-time license fees.

Infrastructure services help provide the functionality for Web services infrastructure management and monitoring in terms of elements such as security and control, asset and configuration management, availability and scalability, and performance and fault management. These tools will include extensive capabilities for reporting and analysis of ongoing transactions, often on a real-time basis. An example is mFormation Technologies, which provides wireless infrastructure management software. Most infrastructure services can be considered applications aimed at the IT department to help it monitor and manage its ongoing Web services operations, both internal and external. Since Web services are oriented primarily toward machine-to-machine interaction, it is critical to monitor and manage these processes in order to ensure that they operate to the required service levels from both an IT and a business process perspective. This can help to ensure that not only is the technical infrastructure performing as required, but also that the business processes are performing as required. As we shall see in the section on business process management, monitoring of business process performance is just as critical, if not more so, than traditional IT monitoring. Another example of a vendor in the infra-

**Figure 2-2** High-Level Web Services Value Chain.

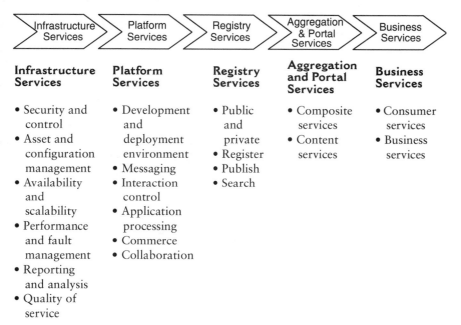

| Infrastructure Services | Platform Services | Registry Services | Aggregation and Portal Services | Business Services |
|---|---|---|---|---|
| • Security and control<br>• Asset and configuration management<br>• Availability and scalability<br>• Performance and fault management<br>• Reporting and analysis<br>• Quality of service | • Development and deployment environment<br>• Messaging<br>• Interaction control<br>• Application processing<br>• Commerce<br>• Collaboration | • Public and private<br>• Register<br>• Publish<br>• Search | • Composite services<br>• Content services | • Consumer services<br>• Business services |

structure services portion of the Web services value chain is Grand Central Communications. The company provides a shared network infrastructure sold as a subscription service. The infrastructure provides process orchestration capabilities in a shared context for business-to-business interactions in addition to underlying data and communications capabilities.

Platform services help provide the development and deployment environment for Web services in terms of messaging, interaction control, and application processing. Messaging may include parsing, transforming, and forwarding messages. As business partners interact, the data needs to be parsed, or checked, for validity, transformed into appropriate structures for internal or external applications, and routed to the appropriate servers. This function is similar to traditional B2B integration server functionality but is enhanced via support for Web services standards. Interaction control deals with business-level activities such as XML envelope processing, message validation, and conversation management. Application processing deals with workflow and integration into back-end systems. The platform provider may also offer commerce services for payload delivery, event capture, provisioning and billing, and collaborative services where human interaction is required, such as customer care. In this section of the value chain, we can include major vendors such as HP, IBM, Microsoft, Oracle, and Sun, in addition to newer entrants such as Bowstreet and Cape Clear. All provide development environments for the creation of Web services-enabled software.

Registry services provide the public and private registries, or databases, for Web service interfaces to be registered, published, and searched. This is where registries such as the UDDI Business Registries fit into the model. An example is Hewlett-Packard, which provides registry services and related software products for browsing and publishing Web services components.

Aggregation and portal services allow service providers to add value by aggregating the Web services components of others and to create composite Web services applications. Additionally, within this section of the value chain, content providers may offer content or information as a service offering, either machine readable or human readable. This part of the value chain strikes at an interesting intersection between Web services and portal software. It is easy to understand why portal software vendors have modified their platforms to support Web services and why Web services vendors are often in head-to-head competition with portal vendors. Both Web services and portal software can aggregate software components to create composite, higher value business applications.

Business services are comprised of consumer-oriented and business-oriented application services. These may be applications such as .NET My Alerts from Microsoft, or their broader .NET My Services offering that was formerly known as "Hailstorm." The application services may be specific to industry verticals or may be functional areas within customer relationship management, enterprise resource planning, or supply chain management that may be offered across numerous industry verticals. This section of the value chain is the final layer in providing an end-to-end solution. It may also be developed in house by enterprise developers.

## Looking Forward

If we look at the current state of the industry, we find that most vendors are currently concentrated on the infrastructure end of the value chain; in most cases, this area has to be well-developed before the other higher level services can be provided. Also, not all elements within the value chain are required in all circumstances. For example, in a business-to-business scenario, two companies may decide to interact via Web services using some of the core standards but without the involvement of a UDDI registry or any form of Web service aggregation from a third party. Aggregation of Web services and the utilization of the registry are optional elements in the value chain based upon business objectives.

There are still gaps and white spaces to be filled within the overall value chain for Web services, but the basic infrastructure in terms of low-level standards and application development tools and platforms has progressed well over the past couple of years. This has set the stage for Web services technology to have a major impact both as a technology enabler and a business enabler. It has the potential not only to reshape business processes but to reshape entire industries—one of the few emerging technologies that is truly worthy of the term "disruptive."

## Vendor Profiles

### Web Services Example

## Bowstreet

*www.bowstreet.com*

Bowstreet is a privately held software company based in Portsmouth, New Hampshire. Founded in January 1998, the company focuses on automating Web application development and Web services and has over $140 million in investment from a long list of corporate and venture capital investors, including AIG, America Online, BankBoston Robertson Stephens, Chase H&Q, Charles River Ventures, Credit Suisse First Boston, Dain Rauscher Wessels, Dell Computer Corporation, GE Equity, Goldman Sachs, Kleiner Perkins Caufield & Byers, Morgan Stanley Dean Witter, Novell, Oracle, and many others.

The company's flagship product is called Bowstreet Factory 5. This is a framework for rapidly automating the creation and maintenance of flexible Web applications.

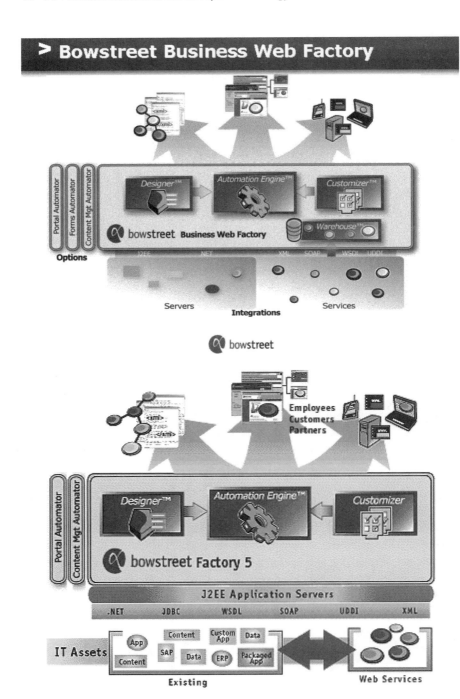

The Bowstreet Factory 5 is a Java-based development environment that consists of three major components:

**Designer**

A tool used by developers to create *models* containing a sequence of *Builders* and to create and modify *profile* sets.

**Customizer**

Models that enable nontechnical users to create, modify, and manage Web applications based on profiles.

**Automation Engine**

A run-time mechanism that can create thousands of unique, just-in-time dynamic Web applications.

Bowstreet offers an open, vendor-neutral solution designed to allow companies to leverage existing software infrastructures and emerging Web services. Factory 5 plugs into existing development environments and runs on common deployment architectures such as BEA WebLogic Server™, IBM WebSphere® Application Server, Sun™ ONE Application Server, and Apache Tomcat.

Bowstreet's client list includes large enterprises such as Cisco, DuPont, GM, John Crane, Northwestern Mutual, Sabre, State Street, and Sun.

# Technology

It is important to look at Web services from a technology standpoint and explore some of the fundamental concepts before moving on to the business scenarios to which Web services can be applied. This should help to add clarity to the concept among the mass of confusing acronyms which do little to explain what exactly Web services are really all about and how they can enable new forms of business value.

The conceptual model behind Web services is a service-oriented view of business applications composed of a service provider, a service user, and a service registry. In the physical world, each of these elements is generally software running on a computer server or collection of servers in a data center. In order for the service user to dynamically search for and discover the software services of the service provider, the service registry is used as a metarepository for information about the published service. A metarepository is a database that contains "metadata," which are basically information about information, or a pointer to the real data. The service registry therefore serves as a machine-searchable database for published services similiar to a Yellow Pages telephone book. It's important to note that this database is primarily intended to be searched via machine, although most registries also provide a browser-based interface for manual searches. Figure 2-3 shows the conceptual model for service providers, service users, and service registries.

In the conceptual model, the service provider publishes component services to the service registry. Note that it is the description of the service, or its metadata, that is published to the registry and not the actual software component itself. These component services can be simple or complex units of business applications, business processes, computing resources or information, all expressed via software. Hewlett-Packard defines Web services as any asset available over the Internet to complete a task, solve a problem, or conduct a transaction, so the scope of what constitutes a Web service is very broad.

The service user, again a software application, locates required services within the service registry and then connects directly to the service provider, another software application, in order to execute the desired services. The service user can execute the service of the provider as a standalone unit of work, that is, a complete application,

**Figure 2-3** Web Services Conceptual Model. Source: Adapted from Hewlett-Packard Web Site.

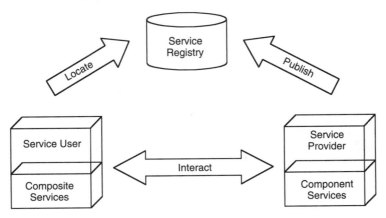

business process, computing resource, or piece of information, or it can combine other services from the same or other service providers in order to execute a more complex, composite unit of work. This conceptual model is very powerful; it describes a mechanism for the business to become a virtual enterprise. Enterprises can provide services which they want to maintain as core competencies and consume services which they want to outsource and acquire from the outside.

Additionally, there is no limit to the number of partners that can be integrated in this manner. Any end-to-end business process can be composed of discrete services from many service providers. With this knowledge of the conceptual model behind Web services, business users can start to think about which business processes they would like to either publish or subscribe to and what kind of value may be charged or paid in exchange for these services.

Web services registries, which serve as the directory or Yellow Pages for Web services, can be either public or private. Private registries are strictly controlled and are typically operated by corporations within their corporate firewall. The private registries are used to integrate with both external and internal services located within both private or public registries.

An example of a service registry is the Hewlett-Packard UDDI Business Registry. This is a private registry that companies can use to create and manage their own ecosystem of Web services. Companies can expose services to the public or they can make some or all of their Web services private and accessible only to selected business partners. When registering, companies enter basic contact information such as name and email address together with their company name, country, and Web page address. Once registered, companies can manage their account in terms of profile and password, search for businesses by name, and publish various services for others to discover and utilize.

The main theme behind Web services is that businesses are now able to use the Internet to publish business functionality and not just content. Other businesses can then search for and access this business functionality, giving them a way to tap inside another business and to execute real-life transactions within the back-end systems of that business. Since the transactions are machine to machine in nature, with minimal human interaction, there needs to be considerable planning in terms of what functionality is published and how this functionality is to be secured and audited. Businesses will also need to understand usage patterns and be able to charge for certain business functions that provide value to employees, customers, and business partners. The Web services infrastructure will therefore need to evolve from the basic communication mechanisms between Web services components that we have just discussed to support a variety of management and monitoring services around this core functionality.

# Business Strategy

Now that you are armed with an overview of Web services, a discussion of the market trends, key players, and some of the technical concepts, we'll discuss how to apply this emerging technology within the business. We'll start with some examples of industry scenarios, benefits and challenges, and case studies, and then move on to discuss ways to apply Web services within your own business.

## Industry Scenarios for Web Services

The following  examples are some industry scenarios that demonstrate how Web services can be applied as part of a business strategy. When considering your business strategy with Web services, the main objective is to think about which parts of your business can be represented and captured as discrete units of work that have value either to employees, customers, or business partners. If you can make a business function into a unit of work that is self-contained, which performs a useful task, and which can be codified via software, then you have the correct elements for exposing this as a Web service. The key ingredients are value, simplicity, and reuse.

**Sales tax calculation.** One of the simplest forms of Web service is a simple calculation such as a sales tax calculation. This is a prime candidate for Web services since it is simple, is something that companies are willing to outsource, and is subject to constant change due to great variety in the tax laws. In fact, there are over 7,000 different sales and use tax jurisdictions in the United States. For example, Hewlett-Packard and Taxware have worked together to provide a Web services solution for the Streamlined Sales Tax Project (SSTP). The solution calculates sales and use taxes on behalf of merchants and then sends the seller's funds and their filing information to the proper tax authorities. It therefore provides two distinct benefits: the tax calculation itself and the remittance of funds.

**Travel services customization.** The travel industry provides another example of the application of Web services. A travel company serving travel agents and large corporate customers can offer a differentiated service by automatically assembling travel provider services, such as airlines, hotels, and rental cars, for corporate customers based upon their travel policies and unique preferences. For example, consider the solution developed by Bowstreet for a leading travel company. The solution was able to bridge various technical systems and business processes across partners and also to be responsive to change in real time to both partner-initiated business rules and customer-initiated business rules.

**Automotive aftermarket portal.** Within the automotive aftermarket industry, parts manufacturers often deal with large numbers of "jobbers" (distributors) and body shops within their distribution chain. This can lead to complex requirements for Web portals that include high degrees of personalization for branding purposes and for the various user constituencies. In this scenario, Web services can be applied in order to simplify application development and to provide the high degree of personalization required due to the various "jobber" profiles and the types of parts that they typically purchase. An example is the solution developed by Bowstreet for a multibillion dollar automotive parts manufacturer which included multidimensional profiling based upon four different brands and eleven types of user access roles.

**Fitness Portal.** Within the fitness industry, a company can build a portal to offer registered members access to training schedules, workout plans, and progress reporting tools. The benefit of developing this type of Web portal via Web services is that the company can partner with other vendors who provide portions of the overall solution. An example is the fitness portal developed by Life Time Fitness, a health and fitness company, which uses a scheduling tool from Xtime, a software vendor in the scheduling software and services automation business.

**Government Integration.**  Web services can be applied to help government agencies collaborate with one another and to exchange information. This can help to reduce silos between departments and to avoid duplication of effort. The integration of agency systems can help to save millions of dollars in terms of IT spending. An example is the Executive Office of Health and Human Services in the commonwealth of Massachusetts. It applied Web services running on the Microsoft .NET framework to consolidate client information running on legacy databases and back-end applications across multiple agencies.

## Creating a Customer Web Portal Using Web Services Technologies

# DuPont Performance Coatings

*www.performancecoatings.dupont.com*

### Executive Summary

DuPont Performance Coatings (DPC), a strategic business unit of DuPont, is the largest automotive coatings company in the world, with more than 12,000 employees in over 35 countries around the world. The company deployed a Web services solution from Bowstreet in a customer Web portal scenario for 4,000 paint distributors and 60,000 body shops. Business benefits included reduced costs, increased customer satisfaction and loyalty, and competitive advantage.

## Company

**Name:** DuPont Performance Coatings
**Web site:**
*www.performancecoatings.dupont.com*
**Symbol:** NYSE: DD
**Business:** Industrial Services
**HQ:** Wilmington, DE
**Employees:** 11,000+

## Challenge and Business Drivers

**Business drivers:**

>> Cost savings
>> Customer satisfaction
>> Market share growth

**Former Process:**

>> Manual-intensive processes such as printing, mailing, and faxing of information such as MSDS sheets to customers

## Solution

**Category:** CRM

>> **Application:** Web portal
>> Product news and specifications
>> Value-added program guidelines and offerings
>> News and press releases
>> Literature, brochures, and datasheets
>> Safety information
>> Promotional materials
>> Approval and warranty information
>> Training
>> Classifieds
>> Color information and color formula retrieval
>> Consulting service offerings

**Technology:** BowStreet

**Target Audience:** Customers

>> 4,000 paint distributors
>> 60,000 body shops

## Benefits

>> Cost reduction
>> Customer satisfaction and loyalty
>> Competitive advantage

### Challenge

DuPont Performance Coatings (DPC) wanted to move its business online in order to better serve its customers and to extract cost savings and internal efficiencies. According to Catherine Marchand, e-Business Strategy Manager for DPC, the long-term business objectives were to use the online presence to achieve competitive advantage and to deliver new forms of value and potentially new business models for their user constituencies. The goal was to make it easier for customers to do business with DuPont Performance Coatings. Additionally, they wanted to help customers succeed since many of them were small businesses with varying levels of technical readiness.

### Solution

After careful planning and discussions with customers, DuPont Performance Coatings decided to focus its Web portal deployment on its automotive refinishing customers, namely, 4,000 paint distributors and 60,000 body shops starting with the United States. After evaluating numerous portal and Web services offerings from technology providers, DPC selected the Bowstreet Business Web Factory due to its ability for mass customization. This was critical since DPC wanted to implement a solution that could serve as a global foundation for all of its business units and brands together with the requirements for unique portal views for its end users. They also needed a solution that could be managed from a business standpoint rather than via custom coding, so flexibility and adaptability of business rules were also high requirements. Finally, another requirement was that the technology provider had a long life expectancy. They wanted a leading edge solution that would still be around in the future.

### Benefits

The business benefits from the deployment have included significant time and cost savings. Online paint ordering is removing some of the workload from DPC customer service agents. Online marketing materials are reducing costs for printing, managing, and distributing paper. Online training registration is saving the company's distributors from clerical work. Online Materials Safety Data Sheets are providing customers with instant access to the latest product information and saving DPC from having to fax to these documents to the body shops. Some of the intangible benefits realized have included stronger customer relationships and increased loyalty.

While a similar Web portal could have been constructed using more traditional software platforms, the leverage of a Web services-enabled platform such as the Business Web Factory from Bowstreet has provided increased flexibility in terms of mass customization, increased business level management of the platform application logic, and reduced development costs compared with traditional software development platforms.

The DPC Web portal site can be viewed at *www.performance-coatings.dupont.com*. DuPont Performance Coatings is currently evaluating the site functionality and adoption as part of an overall assessment phase. The company has found that it is serving well as a tool that not only provides service to customers but also helps determine what customers want in the future. Putting a solution in the customers' hands and gaining feedback are far better than gaining customer requirements from discussions with no concrete solution in place. Some of the lessons learned, according to Marchand, include the importance of looking at the external value delivered to customers, aligning e-business programs with overall business strategy, and performing considerable market research and competitive research up front prior to deployment. Looking at the problem space from an outside-in perspective, and with a no-hurry pressure in terms of rush to deployment, helped DPC ensure that the Web portal met the needs of customers and provided the highest levels of internal efficiencies. The company found that sales and customer service staff were able to provide higher value contact and communications with their customers.

One of the main take-aways from this case study is that solutions can be deployed with early adopter technologies such as Web services with a mainstream and conservative approach to planning and implementation.

## Benefits of Web Services

The benefits of Web services can be divided into both business and technical benefits, as you might expect. The following is a summary of the typical business benefits that may be obtained from Web services:

**New sources of revenue.** Web services allow new sources of revenue to be envisioned as business services are packaged as Web services and offered to customers. These Web services can be fine-grained or coarse-grained as required. The value proposition to the customer is that integration with your business services is made easier and more flexible. It can lessen the requirements for developers from both sides to collaborate on integration standards since Web services help remove the barriers associated with different programming languages and different operating systems. Customers can subscribe to your services and therefore use them with less expenditure on application integration efforts between companies and with more flexibility in how they may interact with your services. In particular, you may be able to offer more advanced personalization and customization based upon your customers' profiles and preferences.

**Competitive advantage.**  Web services can provide competitive advantage by enabling a company to provide services that its competitors cannot match using traditional e-business approaches. This includes the ability to combine Web services from other partners to form aggregate forms of Web services which bring customers greater ease of use and higher levels of service. The competitive advantage comes both from the ability to integrate applications faster and more cost-effectively, and from the ability to create complex Web services aggregations that combine services from multiple partners to create new virtual business solutions and deeper levels of integration across corporate boundaries.

**Business agility.**  Web services can promote business agility by allowing business services to be constructed on the fly. Web services can be mass customized based upon changes to partner and customer profiles and preferences. They can also be dynamically assembled with different partner services or different enterprise services as required for each business transaction. In this manner, the Web services are able to adapt to real-time business requirements and conditions. For example, if a required part is out of stock with a particular supplier, the application can dynamically switch to place an order with another supplier who has the part in stock. It is important to note that while different partners can be dynamically assembled into the electronic value chain on a transaction by transaction basis, each of these partners will typically need to be preapproved as a trading partner up front. This way dynamic business relationships can be orchestrated between known, trusted partners instead of unknown entities.

**Virtual enterprise.** Web services represent a way for a business to move toward the virtual enterprise paradigm by allowing it to dynamically hook into other third-party services on an as needed basis and to expose its own Web services for other organizations to consume. As an initial step, deployment of Web services internally within the enterprise can help prepare for future outward-facing initiatives. If business functions are packed into Web services, they can be offered to various business units avoiding any duplication of effort and can even be opened up to paying customers. An example might be an order status Web service. This service could be offered to various internal departments for sales and support functions and eventually to customers for self-service access to order status over a variety of communication channels such as pagers, personal digital assistants, and cell phones. Another example of an internal deployment would be as part of an IT shared services organization where certain business functions or application services are made available to numerous operating companies.

**Increased customer satisfaction.** By using Web services to aggregate services from various providers in an end-to-end solution for customers, businesses can increase customer satisfaction and loyalty and provide a differentiated level of service. They can also earn referral fees by automatically integrating their business partners into their transactions and referring business their way. An example might be an electronic commerce site that provides automated links to service providers for credit check, logistics, and insurance services.

**Increased productivity and reduced costs.** A final business benefit of moving to Web services for application development and application integration is that the technology can speed development times and provide applications that deal with greater programmatic complexity and variety. In this way, developer productivity is increased and there is a reduction in overall IT costs in building applications using Web services frameworks. Since such a large portion of the business capital and ongoing expenditure is devoted to information technology, this is a considerable business benefit that cannot be ignored.

## Challenges for Web Services

Like benefits, challenges for Web services can also be divided into both business and technical areas. The following is a summary of the typical business challenges that currently surround the Web services arena.

**Strategy.**   One of the main challenges to Web services deployment is that considerable strategy is required prior to any type of implementation. The business needs to determine which business processes to codify into software processes and expose as Web services. In addition, the business must determine which business functions are to be internally developed and maintained as a core competency and which should be outsourced from a known and trusted third party. Finally, business decision makers need to plan which business partners will be included within this virtual business Web and thus permitted to engage in dynamic Web services interactions. Careful planning of business strategy and appropriate business processes for deployment via Web services will be a major factor in determining success. Once developers have learned the basics around Web services standards and platforms, the technical integration challenges will be secondary. Some gaps still exist, however, in the end-to-end technical solutions that are available and developers may need to craft custom approaches to fill in some of these gaps around Web services development, deployment, and ongoing operations. So in addition to strategy formulation, considerable time and effort still need to be expended upon actual implementation and business expectations need to be set accordingly.

**Trust.**   For Web services to take off in mass adoption, there needs to be some form of trust mechanism in place between dynamically discovered business partners. One of the benefits of Web services is the ability for business partners to discover each others' services dynamically for just-in-time, customized business transactions. The issue with moving to these dynamically assembled value chains with new partners is that even if it is technically possible, there are still a lot of business trust issues that need to be dealt with. For example, based upon the type of service the partner is offering, the subscribing business may need to be assured that the partner is competent to do the job within the required service levels. Historically, this has required due diligence, including background checks, credit reports, customer references, and finally, contractual agreements between parties. It basically requires a lot of manual activities to be conducted before any automated transactions can even start to occur between partners. It is likely that two scenarios will exist for business-to-business Web services deployment. The first will be dynamic Web services between prearranged partners. The second will be dynamic Web services between unknown partners. It is likely that an 80–20 rule will exist with 80 percent of the transaction scenarios occurring between known, prearranged business partners. The remaining 20 percent of transaction scenarios will eventually occur between unknown, dynamically discovered partners but will be characterized by low-value-added, commoditized services where trust is less important.

**Security.**   Prior to deploying Web services, businesses will need to develope a clear picture of which functions to expose publicly and which to make private. For those services exposed privately, the business will need to carefully map out which business partners gain access to which business processes and the levels of access granted within each business process. With Web services opening up a huge realm of possibilities for exposing business functions to partners, the complexity of security requirements in terms of authentication and access control will become greater. The business world is increasingly opening up its systems for others to view and utilize, which creates additional security risks and places a larger requirement on careful design and ongoing monitoring of business activities. Since Web services are primarily a machine-to-machine interaction, it will be critical to set up security controls and have mechanisms in place for intrusion detection and for auditing and reporting.

**Critical Mass.**   Web services also need to reach critical mass in terms of the number of business adopters in order to extract the full value offered by the technology. The more business partners that engage in Web services interactions, the greater the opportunity for true network computing, where every business, every application, every device, and every person is a connected node on the network that acts as a provider and consumer of Web services. This critical mass will also enable more dynamic forms of business-to-business interaction as more partners come online with the technology. Just as the World Wide Web enables a critical mass of businesses to engage in human-driven information access and electronic commerce transactions, so Web services may eventually enable a critical mass of machine-to-machine, business-to-business transactions running over the same set of open industry standards and protocols. Of course, business-to-business transactions have been occurring since the mid-70s via electronic data interchange, but Web services will enable these transactions to become more dynamic, more complex, and more real-time with a far greater return on investment.

## Strategy Considerations

Now that we've seen the benefits and challenges of Web services and the various industry scenarios and case studies for how they can be applied, it's time to consider strategy formulation within your own business. Let's explore some guidelines for developing your business strategy around Web services and how to estimate results.

The major business strategy considerations for Web services are which initiatives to target, how to prioritize these targets, how to execute and how to measure results. When determining which initiatives to target, one should map current business initiatives against their risk factor and their suitability for implementation via Web services. Initial projects should have a low business risk factor, should be simple transactions that are easy to implement as Web services, and should have immediate benefits. Low-risk factor projects can be those which are deployed internally or which are deployed to a small group of friendly business partners who are conducting similar initiatives via emerging technology and want to learn similar lessons by working with others as service consumers or service providers.

The business decision makers should look at Web services from several angles. Firstly, they should look for ways to ease the effort surrounding application integration, either intraenterprise or interenterprise. Secondly, they should think about insourcing versus outsourcing. They should think about which business services, exposed as Web services, they want to maintain and control in house versus which ones to outsource to other providers. They should ask which functions can be outsourced in order to avoid a custom build. Thirdly, they should think about ways to generate new service offerings and new forms of revenue by exposing certain business functions as a Web service. In all cases, low-risk pilots and proof-of-concepts are a way to get your feet wet with the technology and learn some early lessons. Web services are more than just technology; they need to be viewed from many angles including IT strategy, outsourcing strategy, and business strategy.

Initial projects can be prioritized by measuring the business benefit gained against the ease of implementation. Those that are easy to implement and which yield high business benefit are the quick wins that exhibit moderate or high reward for low risk. Of course, most of the major wins will lie on the high-risk, high-reward continuum and will require a corresponding amount of implementation effort and business risk in order to be successful.

Some of the early wins for Web services, as we have seen in the industry scenarios, have been in the enterprise portal space, either for employees, customers, or business partners. These portal applications ease integration efforts, handle higher levels of complexity and customization, and yield higher degrees of business functionality and customer satisfaction than prior Web-based techniques without the use of Web services.

A phased approach to deploying Web services can help one move along the learning curve by starting with low-risk internal deployments. It is perfectly acceptable for the first Web services deployed to be internal initiatives that help to create Web applications such as enterprise portals with reduced development costs. The business benefit in this example is simply the cost-reduction element for application development, plus the increased flexibility of the portal and its ability to better manage complexity in interactions and application logic. Web services are ideally suited to complex integration efforts which require integration across disparate operating systems, object models, and programming languages.

After the first phase of internal projects, the business can move on to externally oriented projects with prearranged business partners, and finally to externally oriented projects with dynamically discovered partners. In the later case, this type of interaction should be reserved for commodity services when security, trust, and service levels are less of an issue.

While the business is moving along these phases of Web services deployment, it is important to constantly update the inventory of business processes that are being codified as Web services. As the enterprise is virtualized, it is critical to document and update this inventory of processes since it becomes the digital blueprint for the company's operations. Additionally, reuse can be accomplished only via a thorough understanding of what is currently available within the blueprint. Web services implementations are particularly valuable when there are a high degree of complexity, a high number of business partners or processes involved in the final solution, a high transaction rate, and a high degree of change in business rules and data over time. They are therefore ideally suited to collaborative commerce activities which go deeply into the supply chain for manufacturers, or which cut across numerous sections of the value chain for services organizations.

## Estimating Results

To estimate return on investment for Web services implementations, one can look either at cost takeout from IT investments when compared to other development approaches, or one can look at revenues produced as a result of new Web services offerings. In both cases, the return on investment over the long term can be significant, and for large businesses, it can be easily in the millions of dollars. As the industry matures, it is likely that return on investment models for Web services will migrate from today's current cost takeout focus to a more revenue-centric focus as deployments move from inside the firewall to outside the firewall.

Remember, the return on investment for the business should be measured not only in hard-dollar benefits but also by the hard-to-quantify factors such as increased business agility, increased competitive advantage, and increased migration toward the virtual enterprise. Customer satisfaction and the ability to deliver solutions that were previously too complex to justify are additional benefits of Web services. As in the DuPont Performance Coatings case study, Web services technologies can also be applied to solve traditional challenges such as customer relationship management. A Web portal deployed via Web services technologies can provide internal efficiencies that enable sales and customer service staff to focus on higher value contact and communications with customers, increased business agility, and improved customer satisfaction and loyalty.

In terms of hard-dollar benefits for cost takeout on the IT side, some of the initial figures are encouraging. Bowstreet reported cost savings of over 23 percent in an e-sales portal deployment for a customer in the high-tech manufacturing industry. The cost savings was achieved during design, development, and testing of the solution when compared to an alternate approach using more traditional Java coding tools and techniques.

Bowstreet also reported an annualized cost savings of $1.2 million in a portal site deployment for a Fortune 50 conglomerate. The division of the company on this initiative was focused on consumer insurance and investment products. The cost savings were calculated based upon the number of days saved in terms of development effort and the cost per day in terms of project resources. The cost savings were estimated via comparison with traditional Java coding tools and techniques. In this particular case study, the company also estimated net income of $475 thousand annually due to new cross-sell opportunities.

These examples from Bowstreet show that one of the main ways that Web services are currently being quantified is in terms of the reduced costs for application design, development, testing, deployment, maintenance, and enhancement when compared to more traditional software development techniques. This is an internal ROI for the IT department as opposed to a business-oriented ROI. As Web services mature and enable new business models, new forms of revenue generation, and new ways to dynamically interact with a number of business partners based upon real-time conditions and requirements, we can expect to see this ROI being quantified in terms of both IT and business returns.

The typical assumptions made by vendors such as Bowstreet for the return on investment for Web services include a 20 percent savings in design, development, testing, and deployment of the first application and then a 60 percent savings in the same process for all future applications. Additionally, maintenance is often assumed to be a steady five percent of the initial investment per year as opposed to a five percent annual increase in support costs. With these kinds of cost savings, a return on investment is rapidly obtained.

The challenge, given the emerging nature of Web services development, is to find enough metrics from early adopters and to validate that the assumptions are realistic. It is highly likely that the first few deployments of Web services may actually be more expensive than traditional software development techniques due to the learning curve for developers in coming up to speed on the new development tools, standards, and paradigms for component assembly and application integration. Once this learning curve has been crossed, however, there is a strong case for cost savings in the development lifecycle. Web services help to abstract the often complex integration requirements when assembling portals or integrating different applications running on different platforms. Some of the benefits are similar to those of the fourth-generation development tools and object-oriented development techniques. The ability to develop in a visual environment instead of at the code level and the ability to abstract development to a higher layer of integration, ideally at the business level rather than the technical level, can boost productivity considerably.

Beyond these cost savings within IT which help to reduce overall cost of ownership, additional benefits of Web services include the ability to deal with greater complexity and to integrate business partners and internal applications more rapidly. Service aggregation can also be used in order to create new forms of value by combining Web services from multiple sources to create dynamically assembled value chains from prearranged partners.

A high-level ROI model for Web services is as follows:

*Return on Web services investment = Tangibles + Intangibles = (Increased IT productivity + Increased business revenues) / (IT costs) + Increased business agility*

The increased business agility relates to the ability to create dynamic "business webs" with transactions formed in real time based upon business conditions and to integrate with more partners more easily via the Web services standards for integration.

## Extending the Radar Lessons

>>  Drivers for the adoption of Web services include business drivers such as increased revenues, business agility and cost reduction, IT drivers such as ease of integration and complexity management, and industry drivers such as software as a service, new Web services standards, and open Internet protocols.

>>  The major sections of the Web services value chain are comprised of infrastructure services, platform services, registry services, aggregation and portal services, and business services.

>>  The conceptual model behind Web services is a service-oriented view of business applications composed of a service provider, a service user, and a service registry.

>> The benefits of Web services include new sources of revenue, competitive advantage, increased business agility, migration toward the virtual enterprise, and increased IT productivity and reduced costs of integration.

>> The challenges for Web services include strategy formulation prior to deployment, implementing the required levels of security and trust, and gaining critical mass in terms of business partners all using the technology.

## Extending the Radar Considerations

>> Web services are more than just technology; they need to be viewed from many angles, including IT strategy, outsourcing strategy, and business strategy

>> A phased approach to Web services should include internal deployments, external deployments with prearranged business partners, and finally external deployments with dynamically discovered business partners.

>> Return on investment for Web services should be measured not only on hard-dollar benefits such as revenue generation and cost-reduction but also on hard-to-quantify factors such as increased business agility, increased competitive advantage, increased migration towards the virtual enterprise, customer satisfaction, and the ability to deliver solutions that were previously too complex to justify.

> *Return on Web services investment = Tangibles + Intangibles = (Increased IT productivity + Increased business revenues) / (IT costs) + Increased business agility*

# 3

# Peer Services

*"Peer-to-peer computing is the revolution that could change computing as we know it."*

—Patrick Gelsinger, Chief Technology Officer, Intel

P eer services, or peer-to-peer computing, represent an emerging technology that has a host of potential applications within the business, mostly related to knowledge management and collaboration. Sample applications include distributed computing using spare computing cycles, file sharing, collaboration, intelligent agents, and distributed storage sharing. Peer-to-peer computing allows devices at the "edge" of the network such as desktops to communicate directly with one another in order to share their computing resources without going through a centralized server. The concept of peer-to-peer computing has been around for quite some time, but only relatively recently has it started to gain acceptance as a potential business enabler beyond simple networking of computers, as was the case in the early local area network days.

Peer-to-peer is particularly well-suited as a companion to traditional server-centric, or centralized, computing models and not as a replacement. In fact, the two computing  models can easily coexist within the business environment, providing a best-of-breed solution that benefits both business end users and IT systems administrators. Peer-to-peer technologies have their own unique set of advantages and disadvantages that should be carefully considered before embarking upon collaborative application deployments. While server-centric computing is good for highly structured, controlled collaboration and for information publishing and broadcasting, peer-to-peer computing is good for ad hoc collaboration where end users need to have the control and flexibility to manage their own communications and information exchanges in a more cost-effective manner. It effectively frees the business from the expense of having dedicated systems administrators to manage and monitor collaborative applications.

Peer-to-peer computing presents benefits of cost effectiveness and increased productivity for end users. By offloading the administration of ad hoc collaborative networks to end users, the business can reduce the costs of centralized support and maintenance. Additionally, end users can become more productive by having the tools on their own desktops to create and manage collaborative workspaces and to invite participants to join these groups. This frees them from the time lag inherent in making requests for server-centric collaborative hubs to be created by systems administrators. These hubs typically contain collaborative applications such as content management, discussion forums, and shared whiteboards.

# Market

There is a large market potential for collaborative applications, and peer-to-peer models will probably comprise a portion of this overall market. The Aberdeen Group and AMR Research expect corporate spending on collaboration software to triple from $10.6 billion in 2001 to $33.2 billion by 2004. Collaborative processes represent one of the three fundamental requirements for conducting electronic business: content, commerce, and collaboration. In this market section, we'll look at the evolution of the peer-to-peer computing market and several of the major players and standards initiatives in the space. These include initiatives such as SETI@home and various projects from Intel and Sun Microsystems. We'll also look at some of the drivers for adoption of this computing model within the corporate world and profile a company named Groove Networks, one of the startup companies in the field of peer-to-peer collaboration.

## Evolution

Peer-to-peer technologies have evolved as an additional architectural solution for distributed computing where multiple networked computers are applied to solve a certain business task. They allow intelligent client computers to be connected to share computing resources in terms of files, processing power, and storage space. The Internet and the World Wide Web were originally a collection of computer servers linked together and operated in a client-server manner with information such as Web pages and other documents stored centrally and delivered upon request to client desktops. This request-response paradigm was a natural continuation of centralized mainframe technologies and client-server computing technologies. In all these scenarios, the bulk of the intelligence and control resided at the core of the network at the computer servers. The servers held the data and the business logic and the client machines simply made requests and rendered the content on screen. As the Internet has expanded and an ever-increasing number of devices such as desktops, personal digital assistants, cell phones, pagers, and other smart appliances and objects have been connected, the opportunity has arisen for any device to communicate with any other device and share their resources and information directly without going through a central point of control. A personal computer on the Internet may connect with another personal computer on the Internet, or even with a wireless device. The collective processing power or storage capability can be leveraged between peers as opposed to relying on a centralized server which must handle all requests and scale accordingly as usage increases.

Some of the early landmarks in the evolution of peer-to-peer computing were the peer-to-peer local area networks (LANs) such as Microsoft Windows for Workgroups, Novell Personal NetWare, and IBM peer-to-peer SNA networks running their Advanced Peer-to-Peer Networking (APPN) protocols. All these company examples allowed users on local area networks to share resources on their computers and to access the shared resources of others on the network. More recent and well-known examples of peer-to-peer computing have included the SETI@home project, Napster, Intel's peer-to-peer initiative, and Sun's Project JXTA.

SETI@home is a UC Berkeley program that allows regular Internet users to become involved in the analysis of data collected as part of the SETI sky survey at the National Astronomy and Ionospheric Center's radio telescope in Arecibo, Puerto Rico. SETI is a scientific program seeking to detect signs of intelligent life outside the planet Earth. Internet users can use their spare computing power, when their computers are not in use, in order to process portions of data collected from the telescope. The data are sent to end users' machines as one-quarter megabyte "work-units." Once these work units are processed by the peer computer, the results are sent back to the SETI@home program for merging in a database with the results from other peer computers on the network. The SETI@home program connects only to peer computers in order to transfer data. End users simply download a special screen saver program that contains the logic to perform the file transfers and processing when the local machine is left unattended. The number of users and the total CPU processing time collected by the program are impressive. As of the time of this writing there were over 3.5 million end users engaged in the program over time with a collective CPU processing time of nearly 900,000 years. In terms of computing power, the program has exceeded the rating of IBM's "ASCI White" supercomputer in terms of floating-point operations per second at less than one percent of the overall cost. It has obtained 15 TeraFLOPS ($10^{12}$ floating-point operations per second) as opposed to IBM's rating of 12 TeraFLOPS at a cost of $500,000 compared to $110 million for the IBM machine.

Intel Corporation's involvement in peer-to-peer computing has included the formation of the Peer-To-Peer Working Group, the Peer-to-Peer Trusted Library (PtPTL), and the Intel Philanthropic Peer-to-Peer Program. The Peer-To-Peer Working Group was formed in August 2000 to foster standards and protocols for peer-to-peer computing. The group is comprised of member companies such as Intel, Fujitsu PC Corporation, Groove Networks, Hewlett-Packard, Hitachi Ltd., J.D. Edwards, NextPage, OpenCola, and O'Reilly & Associates. The working group has released best practices related to issues such as firewall traversal, taxonomy, security, file services, and libraries. The Peer-to-Peer Trusted Library is an open-source developers' toolkit for peer-to-peer security released by Intel that is tailored for the creation of peer-to-peer applications. It supports digital certificates, peer authentication, secure storage, public key encryption, digital signatures, and symmetric key encryption—all important elements in helping to make peer-to-peer computing a trusted infrastructure for corporate developers.

The Intel Philanthropic Peer-to-Peer Program was announced in April 2001 to help combat life-threatening diseases, such as cancer and Alzheimer's, by using personal computer processing power in a distributed network environment in a similar manner to the SETI@home program. Additional members of the program include the American Cancer Society, the National Foundation for Cancer Research, the University of Oxford, and United Devices Inc. The number of personal computers participating in the program is more than one million, with more than 700 million hours of processing time already completed to date. One of the programs available to end users is the United Devices Anthrax Research Program designed to help develop drugs to render anthrax ineffective as a lethal disease or weapon even after antibiotics have been unable to stop the progression of the disease. From an end-user perspective, the research programs present software that can be downloaded and run on a variety of personal computer operating systems, taking advantage of unused processing cycles. When running on a desktop computer, the programs either appear as a screensaver or run in the background with no screensaver apparent. The programs are available from the Intel Web site, *www.intel.com/cure*, and are free downloads that are easy to install and run. They typically consume about 50 percent of the free CPU cycles on a computer. The program is fun for end users since it allows them to view the computing statistics of the ongoing program such as top ranked members by processing time contributed and by geography. Users who select the screen saver, as opposed to the background process, can also view graphics showing the current computing tasks being performed on their computers. For example, the THINK-Anthrax project shows graphics representing the modeling of the interaction between drug candidate molecules and a component of the Anthrax toxin. Figure 3-1 shows a sample screen from this program.

JXTA was announced by Sun Microsystems in April 2001. It is an open-source initiative for the developer community that aims to provide a set of open, generalized peer-to-peer protocols that allow any connected device on the network to communicate and collaborate with

**Figure 3-1** Screen Saver from the United Devices Anthrax Research Program Showing Current Processing Activity. Source: United Devices.

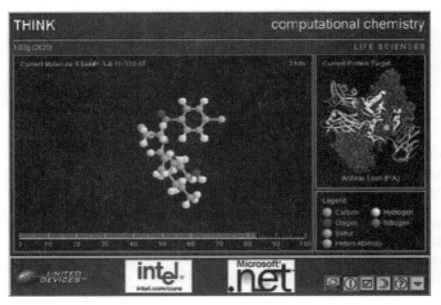

any other. Connected devices may include personal computers, servers, personal digital assistants, and cell phones, among others. The project started as a research project incubated at Sun with guidance from Bill Joy, Sun's chief scientist, and others. Source code for developers is posted at the JXTA Web site at *www.jxta.org*. The code provides three layers of service: a core layer, a services layer, and an application layer. It provides protocols and building blocks for discovery of peers, transport of content through firewalls, creation of peers and peer groups, generic services for searching, sharing, and security, and finally, application level services for file sharing, resource sharing and distributed storage. The JXTA project supports Java as the initial programming language, and, like the Peer-to-Peer Trusted Library, it is helping to advance standardization and ease of development of peer-to-peer business applications that require solid technical underpinnings.

## Drivers for Adoption

Some of the drivers for adoption of peer-to-peer computing have included the rapid increase in the number of personal computers, the increase in their computing capabilities in terms of processing speed, cache, and disk storage, and the increase in readily available broadband networks. The visibility of peer-to-peer business models in the consumer world via companies such as Napster for music sharing was another driver for overall adoption and acceptance because of increased awareness. The promotion of peer-to-peer computing via companies such as Intel and Groove Networks has helped to focus attention on the possibilities for its application within the business world. The increasing computing power at the "edge" of the network has opened opportunities for distributed peer-to-peer computing for the processing of large compute jobs that can be executed in parallel on multiple workstations. The increased volume of information and content on the Internet and within the business environment has also opened opportunities for distributed file sharing and other forms of content sharing. Finally, the increased focus on cost reduction and productivity improvements for knowledge workers has served as an additional incentive for increased adoption of peer-to-peer computing for group collabora-tion for working on projects or meetings with minimized travel requirements. Standards organizations and best practices such as the Peer-to-Peer Working Group and the Peer-to-Peer Trusted Library have helped to reduce the technical barriers for adoption in terms of providing solutions for some of peer-to-peer's challenges such as confidence in the security model.

Value Chain

Figure 3-2 shows a high-level value chain for peer-to-peer computing. As with other technologies, peer-to-peer computing spans the entire computing "stack" from the infrastructure level to the application level. At the infrastructure level, network-based services help to enable peer-to-peer sharing of resources such as distributed comput-ing, distributed storage, and "superdistribution." Superdistribution allows files such as antivirus updates to be distributed to end users using the peer-to-peer network instead of requiring all downloads to occur from a central location. The platform portion of the value chain includes vendors who provide development tools and low-level tools that support peer-to-peer security and interoperability standards. The infrastructure applications portion of the value chain is closely related and includes software for managing functions such as messaging, searching, and publishing using peer-to-peer techniques. The final two value chain elements include technical, or horizontal, applications that support a variety of collaborative functions and business applications that support specific vertical industry functions.

**Figure 3-2** Value Chain for Peer-to-Peer Services.

| Peer-to-Peer Network Services | Peer-to-Peer Platforms | Peer-to-Peer Infrastructure Applications | Peer-to-Peer Technical Applications | Peer-to-Peer Business Applications |
|---|---|---|---|---|

| Network Services | Platforms | Infrastructure Applications | Technical Applications | Business Applications |
|---|---|---|---|---|
| Network Services providing peer-to-peer sharing of resources Distributed Computing Distributed Storage Superdistribution Bandwidth | Operating Systems Development Tools Standards Security Interoperability Peer-to-Peer Trusted Library (PtPTL) Sun JXTA | Portals Messaging Messaging Infrastructure Instant Messaging Search Engines Web Publishing Wireless | Collaboration Knowledge Management File Sharing Message Boards Whiteboards Voice chat Licensed Media Distribution Video Swapping Game Swapping | Purchasing Inventory Control Distribution Exchanges & Auctions Channel and Partner Relationship Management Customer Care Support Gaming |

## Vendor Profiles

As mentioned earlier, the concept of peer-to-peer computing, while in existence for many years in the form of local area networking products, was further popularized by Napster in the consumer space with their file-sharing community for the exchange of media files. It is now becoming an increasingly important technology within the enterprise. Peer-to-peer basically leverages computers on the network "edge" (desktops) instead of centralized servers for performing various content and collaborative functions. One of the major players in this field is Groove Networks, a company whose product lets groups create workspaces to share files, use message boards, mark up virtual whiteboards, engage in instant messaging, have voice chat sessions, and much more. Groove Networks was founded in 1997 by Ray Ozzie, one of the original creators of Lotus Notes in the mid-1980s.

## Peer Services Example

# Groove Networks

*www.groove.net*

Groove Networks, based in Beverly, Massachussetts, is one of the major vendors in the peer services arena. The company was founded in October 1997 by Ray Ozzie, the initial creator of Lotus Notes. Groove's product is a collaborative peer-to-peer technology that incorporates most communications technologies such as live voice chat over the Internet, instant messaging, text-based chat, document-sharing, threaded discussion, and many other tools. The company has received $117 million in funding from investors such as Microsoft, Accel Partners, and Intel Capital.

The company targets a variety of industries and functional areas such as product design and development, purchasing, inventory control, distribution, exchanges and auctions, channel and partner relationship management, and customer care and support. Scenarios can also include disaster aid management, e-commerce, negotiation, merger and acquisition, pharmaceuticals, higher education, and financial services.

One of the most interesting aspects of the Groove platform is that it is based upon a peer-to-peer architecture using XML-based technology. The platform acts as a client-side or "personal portal." End users download and install the Groove client on their desktops and are able to create their own "shared spaces" and invite others to join. They can select from a variety of tool sets to place into the shared space such as a calendar, contact manager, discussion, files, notepad, or Web browser. A conversation tool allows end users to engage in live voice chat that runs over their standard IP network connection. Joint activity tools allow cobrowsing of Powerpoint presentations and coediting of Microsoft Word documents. The Groove software also tracks who is online and who is active within a shared space.

Beyond the collaborative functionality, some of the platform features that make Groove suitable as a robust business tool include its ability to automatically traverse enterprise firewalls by tunneling using standard Internet communication protocols, to encrypt data both over the wire and on disk to keep data confidential, and to provide an open application programming interface for custom enhancements. The platform also supports online and offline usage and synchronizes with other peers when reconnected. Groove's customers include GlaxoSmithKline and Unilever.

# Technology

The conceptual model for peer-to-peer computing is illustrated in Figure 3-3. The diagrams show three models. The first, client/server, is the traditional model of computing where clients, or peers, on the network connect to a centralized server computer for content and applications. This is the basic model of today's Internet where clients are desktop computers running browsers and the servers are Web servers. The second diagram shows the classic peer-to-peer model where clients are all equal on the network and share each other's resources in terms of processing power, cache, disk storage or content, and appli-

**Figure 3-3**   Client/Server, Peer-to-Peer, and Brokered Peer-to-Peer Computing Models.

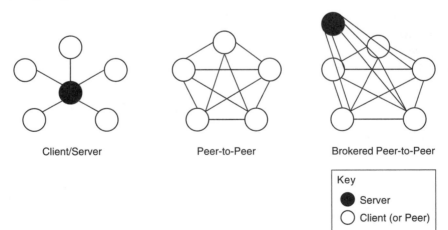

Client/Server          Peer-to-Peer          Brokered Peer-to-Peer

Key

● Server

○ Client (or Peer)

cations. As a consequence of this model, each peer must manage its own resources in terms of security, content management and reporting, and interoperability with other peers. The third diagram shows an advanced form of peer-to-peer called "brokered peer-to-peer." This model actually combines some of the best technical capabilities of client/server and peer-to-peer. It allows a centralized server to broker the interactions and raise the overall quality of service. For example, a server can help to take on management functions for task management and allocation of resources, security, search, directory, reporting and monitoring, and interoperability.

# Business Strategy

Having looked at the fundamentals of peer-to-peer computing and the emerging landscape in terms of vendors and standards, we can now focus our attention on how to develop a business strategy around peer-to-peer with knowledge of various industry scenarios to which it can be applied and its current benefits and challenges. The primary benefit of peer-to-peer is the improved utilization of existing assets, which is something that should be of significant interest to businesses in today's economy. Companies can reduce costs by using existing assets such as desktop computers more effectively, thereby not having to purchase new hardware to support new initiatives. However, the main challenge for peer-to-peer is the security and management of applications. Without the centralized control of client/server architectures, information and transactions are less well-protected and can move around more freely on the network between peer computers. This makes the information more susceptible to loss or compromise, thus raising the issue of security.

## Industry Scenarios

The industry scenarios for peer services break out into peer-to-peer applications for distributed computing to handle large computational tasks, and collaborative applications to facilitate ad hoc workgroups. Some of the business processes that can be enhanced and extended through the use of peer-to-peer collaborative platforms include purchasing, inventory control, distribution, exchanges and auctions, channel and partner relationship management, and customer care and support. Use of distributed computing cycles can be applied to any large computational tasks across a large number of industries. The following scenarios should help to illustrate some of the many applications of the technology to reduce costs and improve productivity.

**Distributing Computing for Engineering Design (Intel "NetBatch").** As early as 1990, Intel deployed a fault-tolerant peer-to-peer distributed middleware capability called NetBatch for its Engineering Design Applications (EDA) environment. NetBatch has enabled Intel engineers to become more productive by using the collective computing power of workstations and systems across the Intel environment both in a local area network and wide area network scenario. This has enabled Intel to gain higher throughput and shorter run-times for their computing jobs and to run more complex jobs. The company estimates the NetBatch initiative has saved it hundreds of millions of dollars. In one instance, NetBatch helped saved millions of dollars in capital cost, by allowing engineers to tap into this global processing capability as part of one of their Pentium Processor (P6X) chip development projects. Without NetBatch, Intel would have had to purchase twice the local computing resources for the project. Over a five-year period, Intel has also noticed that workstation utilization at certain design sites has been sustained at the 70 percent level as opposed to the 30- to 40-percent level prior to the deployment of NetBatch. This has helped to optimize the utilization of existing resources before requiring new investments in further processing capability. It has enabled Intel to achieve more with their existing resources—a compelling story for the adoption of peer-to-peer computing for businesses that have compute-intensive tasks as part of their product design lifecycle.

**Peer-to-Peer Knowledge Management for M&A Activity (Baker and McKenzie).** The law firm Baker and McKenzie used peer-to-peer knowledge management software from a company called NextPage in order to improve productivity for its Mergers & Acquisitions practice. The company is a global law firm with 62 offices in 35 jurisdictions and over 3,000 attorneys. The NextPage Matrix product was used to connect attorneys distributed around the world with the people and information they required in order to perform complex merger and acquisition transactions. Examples of content made accessible by the system includes legal precedents, local regulatory issues, and industry-specific research. The benefit over traditional content management systems is that the application makes content available no matter where it resides within Baker and McKenzie offices around the world. It also helps connect the firms' clients to the business process as they join the collaboration. Additional business benefits have included reduced requirements for travel before M&A deals are signed and the ability to train new associates on transactions via the collaborative workspace.

**Supply Chain Collaboration.** Within the supply chain, peer-to-peer collaborative tools can be applied as an extension to existing enterprise resource planning and supply chain management systems. They can be applied for interenterprise ad hoc collaborations related to exception-handling or other people-oriented tasks that are not well-accommodated by process-centric packaged applications. They help to provide a platform for groups within the supply chain across various companies to converge rapidly to discuss and resolve issues and to store a permanent record of the interactions for future knowledge management. External information that impacts a supply chain process but which is not contained within the core-packaged supply chain management systems can quickly be disseminated across supply chain participants with file sharing, cobrowsing of Web sites, and instant messaging.

**Partner Relationship Management.** Since partner relationship management is highly collaborative and ongoing, it is an excellent candidate for a collaborative platform either based on a client/server or peer-to-peer architecture. Peer-to-peer can help by empowering all participants to make information available from their own machines and to configure the peer groups and collaborative tools they want to utilize. Costs can also be saved in this model due to the reduced requirements for any server infrastructure to be established along with the IT administration requirements. For small group collaborations among many different partners, the peer-to-peer model can be highly efficient. For larger, more institutionalized relationships and strategic alliances, the model should usually be combined with client/server models such as extranet Web sites for greater control over the formal relationship and information exchange.

## Benefits

The business benefits of peer services fall into two main categories: collaborative benefits and computing benefits. The collaborative benefits are mostly related to the business benefits around knowledge management. Applications that are developed using the peer-to-peer computing model can enable knowledge workers to be more productive in a variety of industry and functional areas. Products such as Groove from Groove Networks provide knowledge workers with the ability to create and manage ad hoc groups to conduct business processes in a far richer, collaborative environment than the disjointed phone, email, and fax interactions that are typical of today's office environment. As Groove Networks states, the technology helps people in different companies or different divisions reduce their "cost of connection" in collaborating with one another and performing their work.

The second business benefit revolves around the exploitation and optimization of existing computing resources. As illustrated in the Intel NetBatch example, businesses can generate large cost savings by maximizing the use of their existing infrastructure. Workstations across the organization can be tapped for their unused processing cycles in order to perform intensive processing jobs as part of product design activities, drug research activities, or other intensive tasks such as seismic data processing in the oil industry. The processing power that can be realized from these large connections of peer computers on the network, all applied to the same task, can be far greater than even the most powerful mainframes. This is especially true when the network is opened up to outside participants, and thus a larger pool of potential participants, as in the Intel Philanthropic Peer-to-Peer program and its programs for drug research.

## Challenges

Some of the challenges to the peer-to-peer computing paradigm are similar to the challenges faced by other infrastructure technologies. It needs to gain acceptance by minimizing technology risk and maximizing business benefits. To minimize technology risk, several topics need to be addressed. The main items are security, management, and interoperability. For business audiences to feel safe about using solutions built upon peer-to-peer architectures, they need to have the same level of confidence as they do with their current IT infrastructure and applications in terms of ease of use, security, reliability, availability, performance, manageability, and maintainability. Business users will expect to retain full control over their desktops and be able to fully configure which resources are made available for others on the network and which users are granted permission to access those resources.

Since the challenge is really an information technology management issue, business end users may be unaware of the potential challenges to deploying peer-to-peer computing. As an end user application, peer-to-peer architectures will seem more user-friendly and convenient than most server-centric applications since the administration responsibility is shifted to the business users themselves. It is information technology managers who will have the greatest challenge in supporting these applications. With no central control, or at least with limited central control, they may well be reluctant to allow these types of applications onto their networks. Software companies in this space will need to carefully educate their audiences as to the security and manageability of their products in order to penetrate the market.

## Strategy Considerations

Given the strengths and weaknesses of peer-to-peer computing, the initial strategy focus should be two-fold. First, one should observe where to gain the most benefits from highly collaborative processes. Second, one should look for computing tasks that are highly intensive and which can be distributed in a parallel processing environment. For most businesses, the first area is most likely to be the area of opportunity. Many businesses have collaborative processes that can be enriched with ad hoc peer-to-peer platforms. This can help reduce IT costs and resource costs in terms of IT administration. In an era of focus on cost takeout and performance improvement, this type of solution can enable business users to become more productive without adding costs into IT departments.

The second area of potential benefit for the business is via distributed processing for complex computing tasks. This type of implementation will require a much higher level of upfront planning in order to both identify computing tasks that are suitable candidates and to plan the design of the solution. While collaborative platforms can be purchased off the shelf and are often Web-based—and thus easy to install and configure—the design and implementation of a distributed processing solution for complex computing tasks can be lengthy. The business will need to determine which computing tasks to distribute, which and how many machines to distribute the tasks across, and whether or not the tasks can indeed be run in parallel by a number of machines simultaneously. Even if all these factors are determined, the solution will still require the careful design of a controlling application to send and receive computing tasks among the peer computers involved in the solution and to maintain auditing and reporting information. Businesses embarking on these types of initiatives should look for standards-based toolsets such as those from the Peer-to-Peer Trusted Library or from Sun's Project Juxtapose.

In summary, while the business benefits may be apparent, it is important that the business looks for packaged solutions and standards-based frameworks to target these opportunities. This is far preferable to tackling complex development tasks from the ground upwards with standards that are still evolving.

It may also be possible and beneficial to incorporate peer-to-peer considerations as part of Web services initiatives. Your business may well be engaged in building components of business functionality to be exposed as Web services on the network. If this is the case, then peer-to-peer may enable those services to be available not only to enterprise servers but also to personal computers, devices, and appliances at the edge of the network. In this manner, peer-to-peer computing can help to make Web services device independent and to maximize the usage of all computers on the network and not just server-based machines.

## Estimating Results

As with any other implementation, return on investment for peer-to-peer computing is application-specific, so we will break this discussion into two discrete scenarios: a scenario for collaboration and a scenario for distributed processing.

In the first scenario, return on investment for peer-to-peer collaboration can be determined by measuring the cost reduction when compared to deploying a similar application using server-centric techniques, or when compared to more manual, disjointed collaborative techniques such as phone calls, emails, and faxes. For example, imagine a collaborative hub that includes instant messaging, text-based chat, document sharing, and threaded discussion that is rolled out to

50 employees as part of a six-week internal team project. The return on investment can be determined by the increased productivity of the employees, plus the cost savings from reduced administrative support, divided by the cost of the peer-to-peer platform.

If we assume a $100 per year end-user license for the peer-to-peer desktop software, then the total software cost for the 50 employees in our example is $5,000 per year. We might also assume that, in this case, the administrative support required is reduced from one day to zero due to the self-administration by the participants. Administrative support in the alternate server-centric scenario might include the time spent in setting up user accounts and access privileges and in creating the required discussion forums and document-sharing capabilities. The cost savings for administration might be $1,000 for one day of an administrator's time. This can be discounted from our calculations, however, since the end users will need to pick up some of these administrative functions themselves. Finally, we might assume that end user productivity is improved by five percent, or two hours per week, due to the improved collaborative capabilities of the platform. For 50 end users working for six weeks, this amounts to a time savings of 600 hours throughout the course of the project and a cost savings of $60,000, assuming a $100-per-hour, fully loaded cost per employee. The return on investment in this example is 1,200 percent with the cost breakeven coming after the first few days. When dealing with knowledge workers, the return on investment can be considerable due to the value of their time. Even small productivity improvements can go to straight to the bottom line.

The general formula for return on investment for peer-to-peer collaboration in this example is as follows:

> *Return on investment (collaboration) = (Cost savings from end user productivity + Cost savings from reduced administration) / Cost of peer-to-peer platform software*

In the second scenario, the return on investment for distributed processing is equal to the cost savings from reduced hardware purchases divided by the cost of the peer-to-peer project in terms of hardware, software, and systems integration resources.

> *Return on investment (distributed processing) = Cost savings from reduced IT purchases / Cost of peer-to-peer project*

If the business can realize substantial cost savings in terms of new hardware investments by using existing assets, and the project can be planned and implemented quickly at minimal cost, then there is a good case for a return on investment. The technical feasibility of the project should be examined very carefully, however, since it often requires a complete redesign of how current processing tasks are conducted and raises several new issues for IT departments to deal with. The ability to make the investment last for multiple years is another factor that should be considered. In the Intel example, the NetBatch initiative has been in operation since 1990 and its longevity has ensured a strong return for the company.

# Extending the Radar Lessons

>> Some of the drivers for adoption of peer-to-peer computing have included the rapid increase in the number of personal computers, the increase in their computing capabilities in terms of processing speed, cache, and disk storage, and the increase in readily available broadband networks.

>> The major sections of the peer-to-peer value chain are comprised of network services, platform services, technical applications, and business applications.

>> The classic conceptual model behind peer-to-peer is where all clients are equal on the network and share each other's resources in terms of processing power, cache, disk storage or content, and applications. As a consequence of this model, each peer must manage its own resources in terms of security, content management and reporting, and interoperability with other peers.

>> Brokered peer-to-peer combines some of the best technical capabilities of client/server and peer-to-peer. It allows a centralized server to broker the interactions and to take on management functions for task management and allocation of resources, security, search, directory, reporting and monitoring, and interoperability.

>> Benefits of peer services fall into two main categories: collaborative benefits and computing benefits. The collaborative benefits are mostly related to the business benefits surrounding knowledge management. The computing benefits are related to the exploitation and optimization of existing computing resources.

>> Challenges for peer services include the level of confidence in the infrastructure and applications in terms of ease of use, security, reliability, availability, performance, manageability, and maintainability.

# Extending the Radar Considerations

>> Initial strategy focus should be on where to gain the most benefits from highly collaborative processes or computing tasks that are highly intensive and which can be distributed in a parallel processing environment.

>> Return on investment for peer-to-peer collaboration is equal to the cost savings from increased end user productivity and from reduced administration divided by the cost of the project:

> *Return on investment (collaboration) = (Cost savings from end user productivity + Cost savings from reduced administration) / Cost of peer-to-peer platform software*

>> Return on investment for distributed processing is equal to the cost savings from reduced hardware purchases divided by the cost of the peer-to-peer project in terms of hardware, software, and systems integration resources.

> *Return on investment (distributed processing) = Cost savings from reduced IT purchases / Cost of peer-to-peer project*

# Real-Time Computing

*"There is never enough time, unless you're serving it."*

—Malcolm Forbes

I n a way, real-time computing is something that the computing industry has been moving toward ever since it first began. One of the key value propositions in applying computers to solve business problems is that they can perform both routine and complex calculations faster than we can by ourselves and can therefore save us time. If the task is highly repetitive or complex, we can gain a good return on our investment in the technology. By putting a machine on the job, we can get our work completed faster and go home earlier. In the 1980s, many of us were taught how computers would provide us with a four-day work week and would enable us to enjoy more free time. It seemed quite logical at the time. Twenty years later, perhaps the opposite has been true in hindsight: With ubiquitous information and application access, our data and our work follow us everywhere we go, whether at home or at work. In a way, we have become slaves to the very machines that were supposed to liberate us. As we work with ever-increasing volumes of information in our day-to-day activities, a similar story seems true for the myth of the paperless office. So along with the increase in computing capabilities has come a steady increase in workload, driving us to create machines that are ever more powerful in an attempt to increase productivity and to stay ahead of the curve.

But along with this information overload has come a lot of business benefits as well. As the enterprise becomes virtualized, computers are climbing up the stack in terms of value. They are performing more and more business tasks and are capable of performing complex analytical calculations and routing event-based information and transactions around the world in seconds. The business world has traditionally worked in a batch environment. There were large time lags between the time of data collection, such as store sales at the cash register, and the time of data analysis, such as monthly sales reports. The time between the capture of busines events, their interpretation, and, finally, the reaction to those business events, was considerable. Business reports which historically have been produced weekly or monthly as part of large, time-intensive batch processing jobs within IT departments, can now be produced daily, hourly, or on an ad hoc basis very easily by anyone connected to the network. The computing power exists to generate the analysis and reports in minutes or seconds rather than hours, and the information is accessible at any time. In addition to raw computing power for turning batch analysis and reporting into real-time visibility, the ability to route event-based information and transactions around the world in seconds is also a powerful capability. It has particular merit within the supply chain where real-time supply chain visibility and supply chain event management can provide critical information on the location and status of goods and assets as they move through the global supply chain. This can enable participants in the supply chain to better manage fluctuations in demand, minimizing the bull-whip effect, thereby reducing inventory and costs. Supply chains can also be more proactively managed so that exceptions are detected early and can be quickly resolved before they become more critical issues.

With the advances in computing power and the connectivity of the Internet, business as a whole can now operate on its own schedule and at its own pace—and even faster. The former shackles of technical limitations such as limited processing power, proprietary standards, and distribution of paper printouts due to limited connectivity, which bottlenecked information flows in the past, have been released a long time ago. The real-time enterprise is clearly within sight.

The term *real-time computing* was traditionally applied to real-time operating systems and other areas that required systems that reacted to input immediately and were capable of receiving a steady stream of input data such as embedded computer systems in the automotive, consumer electronics, medical, aerospace, and defense industries. Most operating systems such as UNIX or Windows are not real time because they have a slower response time. Today's definition of real-time computing has expanded to include operating systems, middleware, applications, and even entire business processes. The concept has been scaled up to meet the needs of the business in improving productivity and overall performance. This broader definition of real-time computing is the focus of this chapter. We'll look at how the concept can be applied for business benefit across a number of industry scenarios.

# Market

The size of the real-time computing market is hard to project because it cuts across so many different computing categories, including infrastructure, operating systems, Web services, enterprise application integration, messaging middleware, business process management, business process performance management, and a number of key functional areas such as supply chain management and enterprise resource planning. Supply chain management can be further broken into subcategories that are prime candidates for real-time solutions such as supply chain event management (SCEM) and supply chain decision management (SCDM). What is certain is that real-time computing is a fundamental direction in which the technology sector is moving and one which businesses are readily adopting on a global enterprise scale. Real-time computing can be both an enabler and a desirable end-state. As businesses are able to unbundle themselves from a core competency and business process perspective, they are also able to ensure that these digital manifestations of their business services are moving in real time.

Already we have seen the business trends of just-in-time inventory and build-to-order. An example of build-to-order is Dell Computer Corporation. Dell takes customers' orders and payments and then orders supplies to build computers to the required specifications. In this way, it can avoid carrying large amounts of inventory that may need to be written off if customer demands shift. Moving to real time eliminates a lot of the guesswork or extrapolation that is required when attempting to predict demand. Even in service industries such as the airline industry, companies can leverage real-time operations to manage flutuations in demand and plan their schedules and routes accordingly. They can also offer dynamic pricing in order to sell unused seating assignments close to departure time. In this regard, inventory in the services industry is very similar to traditional product inventory: Both need to be dynamically managed for changes in supply and demand.

## Evolution of the Real-Time Enterprise

As we mentioned earlier, the evolution toward real-time computing and the real-time enterprise has been continuing for decades. Now that many of the obstacles have been removed, the enterprise is free to redesign itself in order to leverage the increased business agility, increased productivity, and competitive advantage that real-time processes have to offer. One of the first industries to adopt real-time computing was the financial services industry and other trading-related industries that rely on real-time data feeds across their systems. Their first requirements for any information technology application are often speed and reliability. Other industries starting to adopt real time now include many consumer and industrial products industries and high-tech segments that have a desire to optimize their supply chains or their retail operations. This has spawned the rise of software categories such as SCEM and real-time supply chain visibility.

Bill Barhydt, CEO of KnowNow, a real-time enterprise software vendor based in Mountain View, California, sees all trends pointing toward an always-on, dynamically configurable, real-time enterprise—an enterprise that concerns itself not only with real-time visibility but with ongoing detection of, and response to, a continually expanding and contracting universe. He sees four stages in the evolution and adoption of the real-time enterprise in the business world. Firstly, enterprises will gain internal visibility of their own information. Secondly, enterprises will add the ability for this information to be integrated with anything, either a machine or a user device, helping to convert the potential energy of information visibility into the kinetic energy of two-way transactions. Thirdly, enterprises will move toward global visibility for their business processes across employees, customers, and business partners. The final stage is when the enterprise moves to dynamically configurable business processses called business Webs.

This vision for the real-time enterprise shows how the concept cuts across so many IT and business functions. It will ultimately help to create a real-time business operating system at a corporate-wide or even an industry-wide level—connecting employees, customers, and suppliers via real-time, dynamic business processes that apply emerging technologies such as Web services to help standardize and provide the flexibility for the real-time integration and interaction. The real-time business operating system can also include a variety of devices and intelligent objects such as those tagged with radio frequency identification, or RFID tags. This will help to incorporate physical objects into the business Web and provide real-time information not only between computers but also between objects.

## Drivers for Adoption

Drivers for the adoption of real-time computing and the migration toward the real-time enterprise include IT advances in processing power, ubiquitous connectivity, and freely available bandwidth together with the business drivers of increased productivity and reduced costs, increased business agility, competitive advantage, and customer satisfaction. Another IT advance that has served as a driver for adoption is the increased ease and reduced cost of application integration. For a real-time enterprise to be implemented, businesses need not only connectivity but also integration into a variety of back-end systems, machines, people, and devices. With Web services helping to ease the pain of integration, companies that previously could not afford to migrate to a real-time enterprise, due to the costs of expensive proprietary middleware, can now afford to do so. The current back-to-basics approach within the economy also serves as a driver by focusing businesses on productivity improvements and internal efficiencies. Moving business processes close to real time instead of batch processing can save time and permit immediate action based upon business events. For example, in the supply chain, being able to provide customers and business partners with real-time information related to the status of goods and assets can provide them with actionable information and can avoid late fees or other forms of penalty. GlobeRanger is an example of a company that provides these kinds of solutions. The company offers supply chain visibility and mobile asset management solutions using data collection devices that include cellular, satellite, two-way paging, and GPS positioning.

Despite technology advancements such as Web services standards and applications helping to reduce the costs of integration, migration toward a real-time enterprise can still be a significant cost for a large corporation. In fact, Gartner has estimated that a multinational enterprise should allocate between 30 and 60 percent of the total IT budget if it wants to develop real-time capabilities. For a $5-billion-a-year business, this translates to between $80 million and $160 million per year for five years. This high cost estimate is probably the cost for an enterprise to get almost all of its candidate business processes migrated to real time. Businesses can, however, pursue a phased approach to the migration to real time and focus on quick wins that can be less expensive. The strategy section later in this chapter will help to explore some of these opportunities.

## Value Chain

The value chain for the real-time enterprise consists of a stack of software technologies designed to perform three basic computing tasks: to collect information, to process information, and to output information. Real-time enterprise applications must be able to collect information from a source such as human-generated input or a machine-generated event, to process or analyze the information in some manner, and then to output the information to the desired systems or recipients. Real-time events can be as simple as moving a data file or data message from one location to another or as complex as a real-time business process that includes complex algorithms for determining the appropriate actions based upon a variety of "what-if" scenarios. Real-time processes can therefore span the entire spectrum of IT infrastructure and applications, propagating through all layers of the so-called "stack." Typical layers in the stack may include traditional applications such as mainframes and databases, packaged applications such as supply chain management software, application servers, enterprise application integration servers and messaging middleware, wireless middleware servers, business rules and workflow engines, business process management software, and finally, end user devices such as PCs, cell phones, pagers, and personal digital assistants. Additionally, embedded systems and wireless communications can play a large role in real-time monitoring systems that can serve as additional data inputs into a real-time system.

In some cases, real-time software rides on top of these existing applications and helps to ensure that the data is routed appropriately across various applications and devices. Software vendors such as KnowNow are a case in point. Their software rides on top of existing applications such as browser-based applications, spreadsheets, or client/server systems and is designed to serve as a real-time router, moving information from one application to another in a publish/subscribe metaphor. The publish/subscribe metaphor is a strong enabler for real-time processes since it allows applications or even companies to become publishers and subscribers to information flows related to various topics. By subscribing to a particular topic, a business can receive all data that is published on that topic from publishers on the network in real time. The vendor profile on KnowNow provides more information about the company and their technology.

Figure 4-1 shows a value chain for real-time enterprise software. The value chain aims to illustrate some of the categories of software that may have a play in the real-time space when constructing a real-time solution. For any particular business application, any number of these software categories may be required. In some cases, just one software package may be all that is required to solve a particular requirement. The main categories include real-time infrastructure, platforms, integration, processes, and applications.

Real-time infrastructure includes elements such as network services for security, management, and monitoring of real-time events and communications services such as cellular and satellite systems. The network services are provided in an application service provider model offering real-time software functionality as a subscription service. An example is Bang Networks, which provides an Application Services Backbone comprised of a set of network services layered on top of the public Internet that enables Web applications to gain the functionality and performance of local area network-based applica-

**Figure 4-1**  Value Chain for Real-Time Enterprise Software.

| Real-Time Infrastructure | Real-Time Platforms | Real-Time Integration | Real-Time Processes | Real-Time Applications |
|---|---|---|---|---|
| Network Services providing security, management, and monitoring Communications Services such as cellular, satellite, 2-way paging, GPS positioning Content Optimization | Embedded Systems Operating Systems Development Tools | Messaging Middleware Enterprise Application Integration | Business Process Management Business Process Performance Management Rules Engine Workflow Alerts/ Notifications | Supply Chain Management Enterprise Resource Planning Customer Relationship Management Data Warehousing Business Intelligence |

tions. Their solution includes a globally-distributed LAN-quality network backbone, network resident application messaging and security services, and Web-native application interfaces. Many of the vendors in other parts of the value chain may offer their software in this network resident manner in addition to offering it as enterprise software that is purchased and installed within the company. Another company in the infrastructure space is FineGround Networks. The company offers a software product called the FineGround Condenser that combines a range of optimization techniques in order to accelerate dynamically generated and personalized content. The benefits of the condensation technology include increased Web performance and reduced bandwidth. The company claims up to 10-fold increase in Web performance from using its software.

Real-time platforms include the real-time operating systems and embedded computing systems that can aid in data collection and monitoring of external factors that may trigger business events or alerts. Intrinsyc is one of the vendors in the real-time platform space making a variety of embedded systems in the industrial automation sector. The platform section of the value chain also includes development tools for the construction of real-time applications. As an example, WindRiver makes software that is used in conjunction with embedded, or hidden, microprocessors that make up over 90 percent of all computer chips sold today.

Real-time integration enables data to be moved based upon business events from one application to another. This has historically been achieved via messaging middleware such as IBM's MQSeries or via software from companies such as TIBCO. Other vendors include companies such as SeeBeyond, Vitria and webMethods; all are positioning their integration technologies as critical enablers for real-time information flows. SeeBeyond provides a unified, comprehensive platform for business integration, enabling a Real-Time Information Network to facilitate the seamless flow of information. Vitria's BusinessWare has been a major player in the enterprise application integration space using a publish/subscribe metaphor for moving data on an information bus. The software has been used extensively in the communications, manufacturing, energy, and financial services industries. Their core BusinessWare platform has components for business process management, business-to-business integration, enterprise application integration, and real-time analysis. WebMethods' integration platform is being applied for global business visibility through its business process management and integration capabilities.

The real-time processes section of the value chain relates to software that is business process oriented. This includes business process management software, which will be covered in the following chapter, and business process performance management software. Many integration vendors products extend into this portion of the value chain as well since most enterprise application integration software is adding business process management as a top-layer of functionality. Vitria's Business Cockpit allows business managers to define, analyze, and optimize their business processes in real time. Likewise, webMethods has a global business visibility workbench that aims to enable nonprogrammers to design global business views. In addition to some of the major enterprise application integration companies offering products in this portion of the value chain, there are also specialty players such as Systar who focus exclusively on the business process performance management field. This field aims to help businesses monitor critical business events in real time and to act accordingly. A dashboard presents key metrics and information that need to be monitored.

Finally, the real-time applications section of the value chain includes software solutions for a variety of enterprise scenarios including supply chain management, enterprise resource planning, customer relationship management, business intelligence, and data warehousing. Sample vendors include CommerceEvents, DemandTec, Nonstop Solutions, PowerMarket, Rapt, Savi Technologies, SeeCommerce, Tilion, Vigiliance, and WorldChain. Many of these vendors such as PowerMarket and WorldChain are focused on the supply chain. Tilion and Vigilance focus on SCEM, SeeCommerce focuses on supply chain performance management (SCPM), and Savi Technologies focuses on real-time supply chain visibility. Others focus on other optimization areas such as demand-based management in the retail industry (DemandTec), demand planning and supply chain management (NonStop Solutions), decision intelligence and profit optimization for manufacturers (Rapt), and automatic identification and data capture (CommerceEvents). Most of these companies have real-time computing as a fundamental part of their value proposition to business customers. They enhance traditional supply chain solutions by adding an optimization layer that helps to manage supply chain events across their lifecycle and to monitor supply chain performance.

## Vendor Profiles

One of the real-time computing vendors that we'll profile is KnowNow. The company's product sits in the integration portion of the real-time value chain and is applicable across a wide range of industries. It helps to provide a real-time solution for moving data across a variety of applications using open standards and common Internet protocols.

### Real-Time Computing Example

## KnowNow

*www.knownow.com*

KnowNow is an emerging player in the real-time computing arena. The company was founded in April 2000 and is based in Mountain View, California. KnowNow sells software for what it terms "integration everywhere," which enables business integration by using the Internet to continually exchange information among applications.

KnowNow focuses its efforts on making integration software that is simple, scalable, and standard. Their software is aimed at developers who are building integrated applications that run inside and outside the firewall. The approach has been to make communications bidirectional, i.e., initiated by either the client or the server. This enables proactive notifications to be delivered to any enterprise application via event-based asynchronous messaging.

The technology consists of three main components: event routers, modules, and microservers. Event routers are server software that routes topic-based events from publishers to subscribers. The routers provide real-time connectivity by maintaining persistent Web connections with publishers and subscribers. Modules provide content filtering, data transformation, content-based routing, and advanced security for the solution. Microservers are used to hold open persistent Web connections between the event router and any application running in a variety of programming environments. They allow applications to send and receive the KnowNow events to the event router.

Typical scenarios for deployment include interconnecting applications over the Internet, collecting, disseminating, and monitoring business data, and real-time enabling of any application exposed to a network. Suitable functional areas for this type of technology include the supply chain, business intelligence applications, and any applications that require real-time communications across distributed systems. The company targets industries such as financial services, energy, telecommunications, and high tech.

Real-time publish and subscribe software solutions have been available from software vendors for several years but have traditionally required extensive custom coding and have been highly proprietary. The advantage of KnowNow is that it is one of the first vendors to address this space using lightweight technology that incorporates Web services standards and common Internet protocols.

KnowNow's customers include PeopleSoft, Wachovia, and Morgan Stanley. The company's investors include Kleiner Perkins Caufield & Byers, Morgan Stanley, Texas Pacific Group, Palomar Ventures, and RSA Ventures.

# Technology

Unlike Web services and peer services, there is less standardization around real-time computing, at least from the broad business-oriented perspective that we are taking within this chapter. While Web services and peer services are technology enablers, real-time computing is actually orthogonal, and is more of a desired end state rather than a true computing platform driven by the vendors. But even so, real-time technologies will probably involve standard Internet protocols and open standards in order to move information and transactions throughout the enterprise in a fast and flexible manner. Therefore, standards such as Extensible Markup Language (XML) for describing data structures and persistent Internet connections between applications and business partners are a key part of the underlying technology. The remaining technology is comprised of the various parts of the real-time value chain discussed previously.

# Business Strategy

A business strategy for real-time computing initiatives should look beyond the buzz words inherent in many software vendors offerings and attempt to uncover real opportunities for performance improvement within the business. The following industry scenarios, benefits, and challenges may help to shed some light on where the opportunities may occur. Migration toward a real-time business is not only a technical challenge, it is also a process and human challenge. Business processes must support the increased speed of information flow and must be able to react with speed as well. The transactions may span computer and human process steps that need to be tightly orchestrated for real-time response. Candidates processes for real-time initiatives include those that can be streamlined to provide better service to customers and business partners, those that can take advantage of time-dependent opportunities for revenue generation, and those that provide opportunities for cost avoidance by meeting regulatory deadlines or minimizing fines and penalties. Real-time processes that can minimize downtime in operations are also strong candidates.

## Industry Scenarios

**Telecommunications.** In the telecom industry, real-time computing can be applied in order to create digital dashboards for monitoring key business events within provisioning, billing, and usage. This can help to indicate potential problem areas and alert managers so that they can respond in a timely manner.

**Energy Trading.** In the energy industry, energy traders can benefit from real-time integration between front-office trading applications and back-office financial applications, helping move them toward straight-through processing that minimizes or even eliminates human intervention in complex business processes.

**Supply Chain.** In the supply chain, real-time computing can be applied to reduce the bull-whip effect by disseminating information across corporate boundaries to improve visibility and reduce inventories. In addition to moving information from business to business within the supply chain, real-time computing can also benefit from wireless technologies for monitoring physical goods and assets. Knowing the location of these items as they move through the supply chain can help to improve logistics and to speed product inventory. For example, American Airlines uses wireless tags and readers from a company called WhereNet in order to keep track of cargo at Dallas–Fort Worth airport. Ford also uses technology from WhereNet in order to track its inventory of new cars after they roll off the production lines.

**Retail.** In the retail industry, demand-based management software can help retailers to better manage their merchandising decisions by providing real-time information instead of dated information from weekly or monthly sales reports. By analyzing retail sales data, and coupling the analysis with real-time feeds, retailers can optimize their over-the-counter pricing strategies in order to maximize profits. Real-time information delivery can help to permit more rapid response to customer preferences and allow closer alignment with fluctuating market demand. In this manner, retailers can experiment with dynamic pricing strategies based upon real-time customer preferences, competitors' prices, and other external events which may affect the optimal price point that consumers will bear.

**Consumer Packaged Goods.** In the consumer packaged goods industry, customers can be provided with real-time information regarding product deliveries. Order status information can be provided to the customers to not only inform them which day their products will arrive but also to provide an approximate time frame. By using wireless technologies on driver delivery trucks, order status can be made with a much higher degree of accuracy based on driver routes and progress during the day as they make their deliveries. In this example, even moving from a daily view to an hourly view can improve customer satisfaction by providing greater visibility into their order status. An example of this type of application is Office Depot. In addition to providing more granular order status information to customers, their "Office Depot Signature Tracking and Reporting system," O.D. STAR, enables drivers to capture signatures upon delivery and to eliminate proof-of-delivery write-offs.

**Financial Services.** In the financial services industry, real-time computing can be applied to help speed the integration and syndication of content such as live market data. For example, a financial services company may be able to collect external data feeds such as live market news and information, combine that data with internal analytics and market research, and then deliver to employees or customers. Benefits of the real-time solution may also include the ability to provide a constant live feed into an employee or customer application such as a Web application, client/server application, or even an Excel spreadsheet. Real-time solutions often hold an open data connection with the recipient in order to accomplish the live feed capability and to be able to push out the data to the recipient. This can often be a substantial improvement from traditional Web server and Web browser connections that are typically request-based in terms of their interaction with the browser making contact with the server based on manual requests.

**Chemicals.** In the chemicals industry, real-time applications can help to reduce costs, increase efficiencies, and increase customer satisfaction. For example, plant operations can be monitored in real time in order to minimize downtime with alerts sent via wireless and mobile devices to key personnel. Logistics operations, such as the shipments of chemical goods via rail or truck, can be optimized via coordination with the schedules and workloads of the providers. Sales staff can be more proactive in responding to customer needs by having access to critical sales information on wireless personal digital assistants. All these scenarios put the right data in the hands of the right people at the right time in order to speed decision making.

## Benefits

**Competitive advantage.** With information available within seconds after it has been captured, businesses are able to make decisions and react more quickly to opportunities that may not exist later on. For example, a retailer with operations on the East and West Coasts of the United States can alter its presentation of merchandise in a West Coast store within minutes after learning how items were received during a new launch at its East Coast store. It can achieve this by capturing data from the East Coast sales registers in close to real time and acting within the three-hour time difference between the two coasts. The Limited is an example of a retailer doing just this. The benefit of real-time computing here is that opportunities can be seized upon that would not be available if the business were slower to sense and respond to its customers' preferences.

**Improved responsiveness and customer satisfaction.** Real-time information can yield increased customer satisfaction and increased opportunities for generating revenues. For example, wireless and mobile technologies can play a role in sales force automation. Using real-time information routing and wireless devices, a car dealership can process customer inquiries from its Web site and route them to the data-enabled cell phones, pagers, or personal digital assistants of appropriate sales agents for immediate follow-up. The increased responsiveness to the customer can help to close business and improve customer acqusition before the competition has even made contact with the customer.

**Increased revenues.** Real-time responsiveness can lead directly to revenues when sales staff are notified of incoming sales opportunities or issues and can act accordingly. Additionally, retail stores can use real-time information to better predict demand on a daily basis and to rearrange their merchandise layouts or bring in new merchandise accordingly. Convenience stores such as 7-11 rely upon highly sophisticated applications that even look at factors such as weather conditions which may change customer buying habits on a day-to-day basis.

**Increased productivity.** Real-time information delivery can streamline processes both in service and product industries. Real-time integration solutions such as those from KnowNow can help organizations to create composite applications that tie together data from a variety of sources. These composite applications can improve productivity by enabling knowledge workers to find the information they need or to conduct various tasks via a single screen instead of taking multiple screens or even multiple applications to achieve the same result.

**Cost reduction.**   Being able to monitor and react to business exceptions can help the business take appropriate actions before the exceptions lead to costly downtime and repair work, increased process steps, or damaged customer relationships. For example, proactive monitoring and remote control of heating, ventilation and air conditioning, or HVAC equipment can help maximize uptime and performance. Service technicians can be dispatched when the equipment starts to operate outside of its limits and prior to more serious issues. Remote monitoring can provide a virtual heartbeat for a variety of industrial automation scenarios. It can help to enable remote servicing and to minimize the number of maintenance visits required by field service personnel.

## Challenges

**Identification of real-time processes.**   Some business processes do not require or even support an increase in velocity. Certain processes have natural frequencies that are incapable of accelerating or do not benefit the business even if they are accelerated. For example, sales leads may come in from an external source once per day. Only if the frequency of the source can be increased can the business move to a faster schedule internally. As an analogy, this has a lot do to with digital data processing theory. A certain frequency has a maximum sampling rate where the data is changing enough to be useful. If the frequency is increased, the sampling rate can be increased as well. Too few samples per cycle and you can generate an aliased frequency that is of lower frequency than the original signal, thus giving a false output. The takeaway here is that if you increase the speed of your external business processes, or if your partners increase the speed of their processes, you need to increase your internal business processes to match these frequencies or risk being out of step. The same is true for the opposite case. If your internal processes are faster than their external process dependencies, then they can be held back and their effectiveness can be diminshed. Any major differences between frequencies, either internally or externally, can lead to misinterpretation of the data. The business can be as agile only as its external sources of input to which it can sense and respond. The real-time enterprise is therefore somewhat dependent upon external business partners in terms of their ability to provide real-time data and to accept real-time data.

**Re-engineering business processes for real-time computing.** Similar to the challenge of identifying processes which are candidates for real-time computing is the challenge of re-engineering those identified processes. The processes may have manual steps between automated tasks that can slow down the process. If these can be eliminated, the business can move toward straight-through processing or "lights-out processing," as it is sometimes termed. If the manual processes cannot be eliminated, it is important to streamline them as much as possible and to seek alternate techniques for encouraging workers to complete the steps in a timely manner. If the manual steps rely on business partners, the incentives can include bonuses for early completion or penalties for late completion. Real-time processes are as good only as the weakest link. When businesses implement real-time processes, they need to be aware of the bottlenecks and have strategies for their resolution.

**Faster operations require more precision.** Speeding up the enterprise also brings increased visibility and increased responsibility. Problems that were never apparent at slower speeds may come to light such as process bottlenecks where data that should be moving close to real time is stopped due to technical integration issues, human approval process requirements, or multiple data entry requirements. Businesses planning to move toward the real-time enterprise in certain areas of their operations should certainly go into the process with their eyes open, i.e., aware of the additional requirements and responsiveness this may place on their business managers and IT operations and staff.

**Managing real-time responses.** Being able to detect business events is a small part of the equation when moving to real-time computing. One of the challenges lies in the determination of appropriate responses. Based on a business event such as an exception, there may be a variety of possible responses that are predefined and even some better responses that are currently undefined. A true real-time business needs to be able to detect not only key events that have business implications in real time, but also to be able to analyze the condition and to be able to react accordingly, possibly developing a new solution as part of the response. For the high-value added exceptions where a rapid response yields significant cost savings, there are likely to be considerable human decision points and a variety of what-if scenarios. This highlights the need for real-time software to include an analysis and rules engine layer to support the semiautomation of these decisions.

## Strategy Considerations

Some of the key considerations when forming plans around real-time initiatives include the identification of the candidate processes for real-time enablement, the assessment of the amount of re-engineering required, the determination of costs and return on investment, and the determination of new levels of performance required to meet the real-time service levels. First, real-time initiatives should be aligned with business objectives. For example, real-time analysis of customer relationship management data may help customer service representatives to provide better service for their most valuable customers and to determine which customers are less profitable for the business. Real-time analysis of this type of data effectively provides customer service representatives with increased knowledge of their customers, their preferences, and their sales history.

There is also no requirement that says real-time initiatives cannot be completed using existing IT infrastructure and applications. If these applications contain the data that are desired for real-time activities, and if the data can be distributed efficiently for appropriate decision making, then no additional software may be necessary. It is important to understand that much of real-time computing simply involves making the right data available to the right person or application at the right time. This can be accomplished using traditional integration tools and legacy applications. Open standards and Internet protocols can help transport the information and ease integration, but the same results can also be gained via traditional tools. In this manner, real-time technologies are often a desirable feature set within existing tools rather than an add-on solution.

The strategy phase should therefore initially focus on key business processes that can generate business benefits from becoming streamlined. Look for hard-dollar cost-reduction opportunities, productivity improvements, or penalty avoidance in addition to the softer benefits such as improved customer service. Secondly, these initiatives should be assessed in terms of their technical requirements. Determine whether the solution can be implemented with some slight changes to the existing applications and infrastructure or whether a completely new set of tools is required. In general, real-time initiatives can benefit the business if processes have a time-sensitive component or a location-sensitive component to them. The location-sensitive component means that information may be bottlenecked in the field due to lack of technical infrastructure. In this case, real-time enablement via wireless and mobile technologies can help to connect the edges of the organization with the core of the organization at headquarters or other business unit locations.

## Estimating Results

The hard-dollar return on investment for real-time computing generally comes from increased productivity and potentially from penalty avoidance, increased revenue generation capabilities, and minimized downtime. Knowing where an item within inventory is located by means of wireless communications can help to reduce search times and to increase worker productivity. Being able to submit data or reports to partners or government agencies within certain timeframes can help to avoid penalties and fines. Being able to react to sales opportunities in real-time computing can help to increase revenues. Being alerted to potential error conditions within equipment or assets can help to reduce costs via minimized downtime. The general formula for return on investment is therefore as follows:

*Return on investment (real-time computing) = (Cost savings from increased productivity + Cost savings from penalty avoidance + Increased revenues + Cost savings from minimized downtime) / Cost of real-time initiative*

The soft benefits related to real-time computing should also be factored into the results. As we saw in the section on benefits, these can include increased competitive advantage, improved responsiveness, and customer satisfaction. With real-time analysis and rules engines added to the real-time infrastructure, the organization can also increase its business agility by enabling a variety of potential responses to business exceptions. The real-time enterprise undoubtedly requires considerable intelligence and flexibility to become embedded into its computing systems in order to extract the most value from real-time initiatives. When this is accomplished, the sizable investments in upgrading infrastructure to become capable of real-time computing can yield sizable returns for the business. For the most part, real-time computing is a high-cost, high-reward value proposition. It requires process change, technology change, and culture change. Since time-based competition is a main way to achieve competitive advantage, today's real-time computing enablers represent a strategic weapon for the business executive to consider.

# Extending the Radar Lessons

>> Drivers for the adoption of real-time computing and the migration toward the real-time enterprise include IT advances in processing power, ubiquitous connectivity, and freely available bandwidth together with the business drivers of increased productivity and reduced costs, increased business agility, competitive advantage, and customer satisfaction.

>> The major sections of the real-time computing value chain are comprised of real-time infrastructure, platforms, integration, processes, and applications.

>> Benefits of real-time computing include competitive advantage, improved responsiveness and customer satisfaction, increased revenues, increased productivity, and cost reduction.

>> Challenges for real-time computing include identification of real-time processes, re-engineering business processes for real-time computing, faster operations requiring more precision, and managing real-time responses.

# Extending the Radar Considerations

>> Candidate processes for real-time initiatives include those that can be streamlined to provide better service for customers and business partners, those that can take advantage of time-dependent opportunities for revenue generation, and those that provide opportunities for cost-avoidance by meeting regulatory deadlines or minimizing fines and penalties. Processes that can minimize downtime in operations are also strong candidates.

>> Return on investment for real-time computing generally comes from increased productivity and potentially from penalty avoidance, increased revenue generation capabilities, and minimized downtime.

> *Return on investment (real-time computing) = (Cost savings from increased productivity + Cost savings from penalty avoidance + Increased revenues + Cost savings from minimized downtime) / Cost of real-time initiative*

>> Soft benefits related to real-time computing can include increased competitive advantage, improved responsiveness, and customer satisfaction. With real-time analysis and rules engines added to the real-time infrastructure, the business can also increase its business agility by enabling a variety of potential responses to business exceptions.

>> The real-time enterprise undoubtedly requires considerable intelligence and flexibility to become embedded into its computing systems in order to extract the most value from real-time initiatives. When this is accomplished, the sizable investments in upgrading infrastructure to become capable of real-time computing can yield sizable returns for the business. For the most part, real-time computing is a high-cost, high-reward value proposition.

# 5

# Business Process Management

*"If you can't describe what you are doing as a process, you don't know what you're doing."*

—W. Edwards Deming

B usiness process management aims to take a top-down view toward solving business problems, solving them at the process level via process orchestration instead of at the data level or application level. This approach is far different from the mainstream technical approach that has been in use throughout all industry verticals for the past decade or more. This new approach is important because enterprise application integration is one of the largest challenges for chief information officers today. A recent CIO magazine poll indicated that enterprise integration software was the most business critical application development initiative for organizations in 2002, beating out customer relationship management applications, security software, enterprise information portal software, enterprise resource planning software, and supply chain management software, respectively. Because business process management takes the top-down, business-oriented approach, it is often a more accurate representation of the original intended business process to be implemented and can help to reduce complexity in terms of application integration requirements.

Traditionally, business processes have been implemented via software as a technical integration issue, connecting systems together in order to complete the required business process. Most business processes span multiple enterprise applications, and the traditional integration approach has been to start connecting applications at the data level or at the application level via application programming interfaces (APIs) or components, using a variety of techniques. These techniques often include custom application development, business-to-business integration servers for interenterprise connectivity, and enterprise application integration products for intraenterprise connectivity. Additional techniques include integration at the presentation layer via "screen-scraping." In some cases, screen-scraping is one of the only ways to integrate with monolithic computing systems since integration at the data level or application level is unavailable due to the proprietary nature of certain legacy systems.

The new approach of business process management aims to put the ownership for creation and management of business processes in the hands of the business community, in addition to the development community within an enterprise. It also takes a holistic view and, in the words of the business process management initiative (BPMI.org), aims to "standardize the management of business processes that span multiple applications, corporate departments, and business partners, behind the firewall and over the Internet." This holistic view also spans people and technology by covering the human interaction elements within a business process in addition to the machine interaction elements within the process. Business process management therefore differs from workflow and groupware types of applications since it relates to both people-oriented processes and machine-oriented processes. Workflow and groupware have been traditionally aimed solely at people-oriented processes.

Although business process management is still a technology vendor-driven approach to conducting business processes, it is certainly a move in the right direction from the perspective of business users. It helps to abstract the underlying complexity associated with enterprise application integration and helps to keep systems integration discussions and analysis at a business level instead of at a technical integration level. The complexity is still there under the hood, but a top layer is now presented in terms that more closely match the business processes being orchestrated. Thus, one of the benefits of business process management is that it makes it easier for enterprise process owners to re-engineer their business processes by simply rearranging process steps instead of requiring deep technical integration changes.

This chapter will take a look at the market, technology, and strategy behind business process management and will also look at other sections of the business process market, including business process performance management. Business process management is one area of the technology landscape where technology companies selling solutions to businesses are finally starting to convert their focus to a business approach and value proposition that is understandable by business analysts, as opposed to information technology developers.

# Market

Business process management is often considered a feature that is added to products in many different software markets such as workflow and enterprise application integration. For example, the Oracle 9i Application Server includes support for business process integration and Web services in addition to its core functionality as an application server running business logic in the middle tier for e-business applications. Because of this, it is difficult to quantify the actual market size for business process management, but the main theme is that this feature is becoming quickly pervasive across a wide number of major software vendors' products. Other software company examples include Microsoft's BizTalk Server and IBM's WebSphere. Both products are application servers that have gained support for business process management via product enhancements or via the addition of acquired vendor products.

Businesses considering integration of applications within their enterprise, or integration of applications with those of their partners, should consider business process management as a key emerging technology, alongside Web services, which can help to deliver new forms of enterprise agility and reduction of cost and complexity. As Web services expose business functionality as discrete services, business process management techniques can help business analysts to shape the business rules around how these services interoperate.

## Evolution

One of the key events in the business process management market evolution has been the formation of the business process management initiative, or BPMI.org. This is a nonprofit corporation whose mission is to "promote and develop the use of business process management through the establishment of standards for process design, deployment, execution, maintenance, and optimization." BPMI.org was formed in August 2000 by a group of 16 enterprise software vendors and consulting firms. It is chaired today by Computer Sciences Corporation and Intalio Inc. The initiative has produced a metalanguage for the modeling of business processes called Business Process Modeling Language (BPML). BPML was first released to the public in March 2001. Together with Business Process Query Language (BPQL), these two open specifications are aimed to support the management of business processes via business process management systems (BPMS) in a similar fashion to the way that structured query language (SQL) and relational database management systems (DBMS) support the management of business data.

Today it is unthinkable to design a business application without the use of a relational database management system in order to represent and store the data elements of the application. In the future, it may also be reasonable to apply a business process management system for the representation and storage of business processes. One of the advantages to this method is that business processes stored in this manner can be more easily executed and maintained. A change in business process can be made more easily since the overarching business processes have been extracted from the core business logic and can be changed without substantial code changes.

## Drivers for Adoption

One of the drivers for adoption of business process management has been the general convergence of business and technology as inseparable functions within the enterprise over the last several years. As information technology has raised its strategic value to the business and has changed from a support function, to a business enabler, to a business unto itself, it has begun to adapt to business approaches. Information technology departments have increasingly articulated their value to the business audience by using common business terminology and valuation mechanisms. The rise of business process management is another example of information technology adapting to become more accessible and acceptable to business users.

In addition, business process management is a new form of business re-engineering. Instead of a one-time event, it allows the design and management of business processes to become continual events that can be shaped and adjusted as dictated by business conditions. In this manner, it can improve business agility by offering an effective way to reshape business processes and make changes on the fly. By extracting the process aspects of a business function from the code that executes the function, business owners can better optimize their functions and experiment until the maximum efficiencies are obtained.

As more and more enterprise processes have been codified via software over the past several years, flexibility has become an important issue and a problem area. Now that the business has implemented enterprise resource planning, supply chain management, and customer relationship management packages, the new mandate is to ensure that these systems are flexible. According to Ray Lane, a venture capitalist with Kleiner Perkins, Caufield & Byers, and former President and Chief Operating Officer of Oracle Corporation, many of these investments in enterprise packaged applications resulted in only a 20 percent return on the anticipated value. He sees automation software, which includes the business process management category, as a key enabler over the next several years for realizing the remaining 80 percent return on anticipated value.

## Vendor Profiles

Vendors in the business process management space, or involved with BPMI.org include a number of enterprise application integration and business-to-business integration software vendors and other types of providers, including ATG, Asera, BEA, BMC Software, Bowstreet, Commerce One, CrossWorlds, Epicentric, Excelon, Extricity, FileNet, Fuego, HP, IBM, Intalio, Intraspect, Jamcracker, Level 8, Mercator, PeopleSoft, Rational, SAP, SeeBeyond, SilverStream, Sterling Commerce, Sun Microsystems, Sybase, Systar, Taviz, Tibco Software, Vignette, Vitria, and webMethods.

In addition to the integration level providers, there are companies specializing in business process outsourcing and in various business process management software niches. Zaplet is an example of a software vendor in a specialist role. The company offers the Zaplet *App-*

*mail System* which is collaborative business process management software that leverages a user's email inbox in order to deliver application functionality to complete business processes. Organizations such as the CIA are using Zaplet's technology in order to deploy collaborative applications that bridge the gap between machine-centric, structured enterprise applications and human-centric, unstructured email. This allows end users to interact with critical enterprise processes from the familiar and user-friendly email environment.

One of the founders of the business process management initiative is a company called Intalio. It therefore makes sense to profile them as an example software vendor in the space. The discussion below provides some background information on the company and their products and services.

## Business Process Management Example

### Intalio

*www.intalio.com*

Intalio is a privately held software company based in San Mateo, California. The company was founded in July 1999 and its investors include the Woodside Fund and 3i Technology Ventures.

Intalio focuses exclusively on business process management and offers a product called Intalio n3, which was the first standards-based BPMS. Businesses can use the Intalio n3 BPMS in order to design, deploy, execute, maintain, and optimize processes such as on-demand design and manufacturing, collaborative supply-chain execution, end-to-end telecommunications services provisioning, or electronic banking.

The n3 product contains a series of tools to help business analysts and developers through the entire lifecycle of business process management from design, to deployment and execution, and finally to maintenance and optimization. The n3 Designer allows business processes to be designed in a graphical manner and the n3 Repository allows business processes to be converted to BPML code and stored for later execution by the n3 Server. The n3 Console allows systems administrators to ensure the reliability, scalability, and security of business processes in execution and, finally, the n3 Optimizer can be used to detect and solve bottlenecks and inefficiencies in process designs.

# Technology

The concepts behind business process management are best described in terms of the standards developed by BPMI.org. The core component of the system is the BPMS. This can be thought of as a database for business processes in much the same way that a relational database management system is a database for enterprise data. The standard for querying business processes is BPQL, which is analogous to SQL in the traditional database world. Finally, the language for modeling business processes is BPML.

Since a business process management system is an engine for business services orchestration, it must be able to integrate with a number of enterprise infrastructure and application components. These can include messaging systems, application servers, object request brokers, transaction processing monitors, databases, and a number of enterprise packaged applications. While some of these systems may be unfamiliar to the business stakeholder, the main takeaway is that a BPMS serves as a top layer of integration that can help to separate business process from business application logic and can help to orchestrate these business processes across applications, users, and devices. In performing this orchestration, there will be numerous touch-points to both people and applications. The amount of effort in implementing these touch-points will be highly dependent on the particular BPMS and the complexity of the business process in question. The business process management approach is not a magic bullet in terms of ease of integration, but offers a new paradigm with benefits such as increased agility and reduced cost of ownership, as discussed later in this chapter.

# Business Strategy

## Industry Scenarios

Business process management can be applied to a number of functional areas within the enterprise in a number of industries. Common industries for this type of solution include those where there are requirements for dynamic and complex business processes such as within the energy industry, financial services industry, and the telecommunications industry. Typical functional areas include customer relationship management, enterprise resource planning, and supply chain management.

## Benefits

The business benefits for business process management include the establishment of a holistic approach that includes people, process and technology, increased agility, reduction of complexity, decreased cost of ownership, and faster return on investment. These business benefits can be both tangible and intangible in terms of how they contribute toward a traditional return on investment. Reduced cost of ownership and operational efficiencies can yield measurable returns on investment, but benefits such as increased agility, although harder to quantify, are equally significant. In fact, some of the strongest benefits of business process management relate to the ability to monitor business processes in real time and to be able to change or redesign the process steps as business conditions dictate. Another benefit is that the knowledge behind the business processes that relates to their design and usage is captured in an electronic system of record. This system of record is similar in approach to the way in which relational database designs are captured in a database management system such as Oracle.

**Holistic approach.**   One of the main benefits of business process management is that it can enable a holistic approach to solving business problems that incorporates people, process, and technology and can span multiple enterprise boundaries. It is most relevant for complex, lengthy processes that involve numerous applications and business partners and are of high business value. Traditional application integration techniques embed business processes deeply into the code level and are often hard to modify. Traditional techniques also often fail to incorporate the human side of a business process and the full end-to-end considerations across multiple applications or business partners.

**Increased agility.**   By managing business processes from the top down, businesses can gain considerable agility in terms of being able to modify and optimize their business processes on the fly. As application and business functionality becomes exposed as Web services components, business process orchestration can be used to execute the high-level business rules related to their interaction with other partner Web services. Both public and private business processes can be orchestrated in order to complete business transactions. Public processes are those processes made available for partners, whereas private processes are those that are kept internal and are hidden from outside view.

**Reduced complexity.** For the business analyst who is involved in process design, deployment, execution, maintenance, and optimization, the complexity of applications is greatly reduced since the view is abstracted to the process level. The business analyst can view process nodes as "black boxes" that execute required elements of functionality without having to be concerned with the technical details of their inner workings.

**Decreased cost of ownership.** Cost of ownership is reduced with business process management, since changes can ideally be made via changes to business process within the business process management system—a database storing the defined business processes. This is far simpler than having to make changes to application code and then having to compile the code and issue new versions.

**Faster return on investment.** In certain cases, when a solid IT infrastructure is already in place, business process management can be applied as a wrapper around existing business applications in order to manage the business rules related to interaction. This can generate a fast return on investment when compared to traditional application development or integration.

## Challenges

The challenges for business process management include making the shift from a technology-oriented to a process-oriented approach, the abstraction of business processes from business logic for true agility, the packaging of business logic for modularity, and enterprise training and change management for employees.

**Making the paradigm shift from IT integration to process integration.** Business process management is a new paradigm for the development and deployment of business applications. As such, there is a paradigm shift for the organization to embrace before the benefits can be fully realized. Since the process can be very different from traditional application integration solutions, a gradual approach via low-risk pilot projects can help to build confidence and early successes.

**Abstraction of business process from business logic.**    To gain the most benefits from business process management, the business logic, in terms of the specific business functions and calculations that need to be performed, must be abstracted from the overarching business process orchestration. Business logic can be thought of as the software code that completes specific business functionality such as calculations or database updates. Business processes can be flexible and adaptable only if the process steps are uncoupled from this type of business logic. When business process steps are too tightly coupled with business logic, they become hard-coded into software executables and can be adjusted only via complete rewrites of the applications. Such rewrites often take weeks or months. The best candidate business scenarios for business process management are therefore megaprocesses that span a large number of smaller application modules that not do require adjustment and are self-contained.

**Componentization of business logic.**    To achieve the abstraction of business process from business logic, the business logic must become componentized and loosely coupled. It needs to become more granular in its organization and easily integrated with other components via well-defined interfaces. For legacy applications such as mainframe and client/server systems, this is often not the case. These applications tend to be monolithic in nature, holding large amounts of presentation logic, business logic, and data logic in single executable files. For business process management to be most effective, business logic must be neatly packaged into discrete elements that can easily be orchestrated and invoked in a variety of sequences for process optimization.

**Training and change management.**    One of the challenges in implementing business process management is that new user roles need to be defined during development and deployment. Business applications have historically been implemented by an IT-centric approach using technology-oriented analysts and developers. Ongoing maintenance has been conducted by IT administrators and operations staff. End-user involvement from the business side has historically been confined to initial input into requirements and then actual usage of the final application. The business process management approach pulls business users into the lifecycle of the application more heavily. It uses business analysts to define and orchestrate business processes as part of the overall solution development and operations. These business analysts must be trained to use the new toolsets and must maintain an ongoing job function in order to manage and continuously optimize the processes of their organization. Training and change management are therefore amplified for organizations considering business process management initiatives when compared to traditional IT application development or package implementation initiatives. The result, however, is greater business control over the solution.

## Strategy Considerations

Business process management should be considered an ongoing initiative that contributes toward process excellence. It provides the business with a way to manage the entire process lifecycle from modeling, to testing and deployment, and finally to monitoring and optimization. It should therefore be approached with considerable upfront planning in order to define both the initial integration aspects and the ongoing management and monitoring aspects.

The best candidates for business process management are long-running, complex transactions that span a number of business partners. These transactions can often run for days or weeks and have complex processing requirements in terms of state management and exception handling. They can occur in most industries, including financial services, insurance, telecommunications, and manufacturing. They are often megaprocesses that include a number of individual applications. Business process management can help to optimize the process steps involved and to provide a dashboard for continual monitoring of processes while in execution. As such, business process management represents a new way to manage these long-running transactions and requires considerable end-user training and change management.

A strategy around business process management should first aim to determine which business processes are the best candidates for implementation. Before implementing a solution, the selected business processes should be analyzed in terms of efficiency and bottlenecks. Many manual process steps may be able to be automated through redesign of the business process at the design stage prior to implementing the business process management solution.

Internal projects are usually the safest early initiatives for implementation. Such projects might relate to a variety of internal workflows around customer relationship management or enterprise resource planning. Once the business has adapted to the paradigm shift in terms of business process integration versus traditional application integration, which will typically still be an underlying layer, you can start to think about how business processes may be exposed for others to utilize. As software components and elements of functionality become exposed on the internal or external network as services, you can think of the business process management system as a powerful tool to help you orchestrate these services and define the rules of engagement.

Business process management is actually affecting not only software companies in the integration marketplace but also within the service provider marketplace. Traditional ASPs and business process outsourcers are starting to think about how they can become business process providers. Instead of hosting an application such as enterprise resource planning, or a business process such as payroll, they can now serve as external business process orchestrators or business services providers. In this manner, they can help to manage megaprocesses between organizations who do not want to maintain these process competencies themselves. With the emergence of Web services, these companies can also outsource complex business processes that span multiple businesses and multiple applications that were previously too complex and too proprietary to tackle.

An example company in this space is Exigen. The company offers what they call a business process utility, or BPU, which allows companies to lower their total cost of ownership by outsourcing their critical but nondifferentiating business processes. Sample verticals and business processes that are candidates for this type of business process utility service include mortgage and loan processing in the banking industry, policy origination and claims processing in the insurance industry, and broadband service provisioning in the telecommunications industry.

A strategy for business process management should therefore consider which processes are candidates for outsourcing and which are most desirable for maintaining as an internal core competency. Critical processes that are nondifferentiating can be outsourced, providing that the service provider has the necessary track record and financial stability to become a trusted partner.

## Estimating Results

Estimation of results related to business process management is highly application- and industry-dependent, but in general it allows business processes to be streamlined. Business processes can be modeled, deployed, and managed more effectively with a business process management system in place. This can improve customer loyalty and lower operating costs. It will be easier to deploy new applications and to make changes to existing applications using a BPMS in the same way that a relational database management system (RDBMS) such as Oracle helps with data design and management. In this manner, the total cost of ownership is reduced substantially when deploying complex processes throughout the organization. There are IT cost savings from using the BPMS for initial design, and business cost savings from using the system in operation. Increased revenues can result from being able to more closely match process steps with changing business requirements. The general formula for return on investment is therefore as follows:

> *Return on investment (business process management) =*
> *(IT cost savings from business process management system*
> *+ Cost savings from improved business process*
> *management + Increased revenues) / Cost of business*
> *process management initiative*

The soft benefits for business process management, once again, are related to improved customer loyalty, increased process agility, reduced complexity, and a holistic approach to solving business problems that more closely fits the business requirements.

# Extending the Radar Lessons

>> Business process management aims to take a top-down view toward solving business problems, solving them at the process level via process orchestration instead of at the data level or application level.

>> One of the drivers for adoption of business process management has been the general convergence of business and technology as inseparable functions within the enterprise over the last several years.

>> The business benefits for business process management include the establishment of a holistic approach that includes people, process and technology, increased agility, reduction of complexity, decreased cost of ownership, and faster return on investment.

>> The challenges for business process management include making the shift from a technology-oriented to a process-oriented approach, the abstraction of business processes from business logic for true agility, the packaging of business logic for modularity, and enterprise training and change management for employees.

# Extending the Radar Considerations

>> Business process management should be considered to be an ongoing initiative that contributes toward process excellence. It provides the business with a way to manage the entire process lifecycle from modeling, to testing and deployment, and finally to monitoring and optimization.

>> A strategy for business process management should consider which processes are candidates for outsourcing and which are most desirable for maintaining as an internal core competency.

> *Return on investment (business process management) =*
> *(IT cost savings from business process management*
> *system + Cost savings from improved business process*
> *management + Increased revenues) / Cost of business*
> *process management initiative*

# 6

# Mobile Business

*"The only way to discover the limits of the possible is to go beyond them into the impossible."*

—Arthur C. Clarke

I n this chapter, we will look at some of the emerging applications in the field of mobile business beyond the wireless enablement of enterprise packaged applications such as customer relationship management, enterprise resource planning, and supply chain management. We'll look at categories including wireless infrastructure management, mobile commerce, location-based services, telematics, and electronic tagging. Before launching into these emerging categories it is worth looking briefly at the history of mobile computing in order to see how it began and how it has paved the way for today's solutions.

In the first generation of mobile computing over the last decade or so, devices, networks, and applications were highly proprietary and consisted of mostly closed systems that performed targeted functions for mobile workers such as bar-code scanning and data entry. During this period, the industry also experienced several misfires in terms of pen-based computing and other technologies such as handwriting recognition which did not take off as expected among consumers. The Apple Newton OS-based products such as the MessagePad were introduced in 1993 and helped to create the personal digital assistant market. They were later discontinued in 1998 in order for Apple to focus resources on the Macintosh operating system. Despite this change in direction, these products helped to promote affordable mobile computing in the industry and were simply ahead of their time. Features included handwriting recognition and communications capabilities such as fax and email support even with the first MessagePad, the OMP, which was launched in 1993 at MacWorld, Boston. Overall, these early products helped pave the way for future PDAs such as the Palm Pilot and Windows CE devices to follow in the years ahead. These newer devices benefited from the increases in processing power over time due to Moore's Law, which helped manufacturers implement desirable features for consumers at an ever more affordable price.

The second generation of mobile computing really started in the late 1990s during the height of the dot-com era and the e-business era. From an enterprise perspective, this marked the start of a focus on extending enterprise applications so that mobile workers had access from the field and on providing mobile access to email and personal information management functionality. Also apparent during that timeframe was the move toward more open standards for wireless data such as the wireless application protocol and other Internet-based protocols.

Today, we are entering the third generation of mobile computing, which contains the market sectors mentioned earlier: wireless infrastructure management, mobile commerce, location-based services, telematics, and electronic tagging. This list of market sectors is by no means exhaustive and simply represents a sampling of some of the more interesting directions that mobile computing is taking as it evolves. These directions promise to more fully exploit the true benefits of mobility across both humans and machines by making mobile computing ubiquitous and embedded into our everyday activities and operations.

In order to exploit these new benefits of mobility in this third generation of mobile computing, one of the first items that is required, after the basics such as increased wireless bandwidth and geographic coverage, is a solid foundation for wireless infrastructure management. This can enable the enterprise or carriers to better manage the proliferation of devices, applications, and users from a security, management, and monitoring perspective.

The next sector, mobile commerce, provides the opportunity for ubiquitous electronic commerce transactions unconfined by physical location or access device. Location-based services can provide the location overlay and thus the added intelligence to information and transactions. This is especially important within the enterprise supply chain, or within consumer applications, helping to locate and track people and assets. Telematics can provide information, communications, and entertainment to automobiles. From a consumer standpoint, telematics stands to make the automobile the second most important convergence platform for digital services after the home.

Wearable devices help to adapt computer systems around the way that we work rather than requiring us to adapt ourselves and our movements around machines. They help to eliminate the additional process steps which take us away from the point of business activity in order to perform data entry or lookup tasks. Wearable devices can also help to create an augmented reality where digital information is superimposed upon the view of our physical surroundings. In this way, it enhances the physical reality rather than trying to replace it with complete virtual reality. The applications for augmented reality are numerous, and academic institutions such as the Columbia University Computer Graphics and User Interfaces Lab are creating exciting experimental systems. Applications for augmented reality can include military operations, field service and repair, medicine, and consumer-oriented applications that provide additional information about a user's surroundings.

Embedded computing enables machine-to-machine interaction from an industrial automation perspective and has great significance for consumer and industrial products and for remote management of a wide variety of devices and equipment. Electronic tagging via techniques such as RFID enables objects to gain intelligence, or to at least identify themselves via a unique identification number, and provide information back to the network regarding their key attributes.

Within several of these emerging areas, we'll discuss the technology and how it can be applied in business scenarios that are just starting to appear and be adopted for new forms of value creation. Some of these solutions have been in place for several years but have been subject to expensive, proprietary technologies or business barriers that have hindered widespread adoption. Today, many of these barriers are coming down. For example, RFID chips are becoming smaller and cheaper and the industry is starting to standardize with initiatives such as the Auto-ID Center, an industry-funded research program at M.I.T. The Auto-ID Center has a goal "to change the way we exchange information and products by merging bits (computers) and atoms (everyday life) in a way that dramatically enhances daily life in the all inclusive global arena of supply and demand—the supply chain."

The emergence of more open standards and the reduction in costs for many of these technologies have served to create the market and initial trigger for both consumer and enterprise adoption. Along with Web services, the mobile business technologies discussed here are key disruptive technologies that should be on the radar of most enterprises. They can be applied across industry in a variety of scenarios for revenue generation, performance improvement, and cost reduction.

# Wireless Infrastructure Management

Wireless infrastructure management is a key requirement prior to any form of large-scale enterprise deployment of mobile or wireless technologies. It can help reduce costs of operation and to ensure the best possible return on investment from mobile enterprise initiatives. As more and more devices and applications are deployed to mobile workers, the enterprise must take more control in order to standardize the environment and to minimize support and maintenance costs. Control is critical due to the maze of devices, operating systems, wireless networks, standards, and applications that comprise wireless or mobile solutions. In comparison, the wired corporate environment is fairly homogeneous, at least from the end-user perspective, consisting of standardized network technologies, PCs, and operating systems. A challenge with wireless and mobile devices is that they have often entered usage within the enterprise as employee-owned devices which are unsupported by enterprise IT departments. Devices such as the iPAQ and Palm are increasingly used for mobile access to personal information management data such as calendar and address book functionality and are often synchronized on an ad hoc basis by employees. Some employees have taken an additional step beyond simple synchronization by connecting their devices to the Internet via wireless modems. When issues are encountered with these devices or with network connectivity, employees are increasingly looking to enterprise IT departments for support since the device is now critical to their business activities.

From a strategy perspective, the enterprise has two choices when it comes to supporting wireless and mobile devices: to continue to allow the proliferation of unsupported employee devices and applications running over a variety of networks or to begin to rein in the technology and move toward standardization. While this may require an initial upfront investment in providing devices, air time, and supporting and maintaining applications, the long-term benefits to the business are clear. They include reduced long-term support costs, ability to roll out new applications faster and more pervasively across the work force, increased end-user productivity, and increased security for enterprise data. The increase in end-user productivity is critical. In fact, Gartner estimates that lost productivity caused by handheld device technical problems could cost the average Fortune 500 corporation about $5 million per year.

Wireless infrastructure management platforms typically include control and security capabilities, real-time performance management and fault localization capabilities, and asset and configuration management capabilities. Devices must be inactivated if they are lost or stolen. This function can include temporarily or permanently locking the device from unauthorized access to information, deletion of all or a portion of the content residing on the device, or remote management of passwords and security policies. This type of management capability can help prevent accidental losses of devices from turning into significant security vulnerabilities. On the support side, technical problems need to be detected in real time and localized in terms of finding the source of the problem. This can aid support staff in diagnosing problems and fixing them as promptly as possible. An end-to-end performance view can aid in this fault localization by highlighting bottlenecks in data transmission or connectivity problems. Finally, on the configuration management side, the enterprise needs an up-to-date picture of usage activity and the devices and applications assigned to each user. This can help to show how and where wireless devices are being utilized and can also provide real-time device data such as available memory, battery level, password status, and device status for problem resolution.

One of the vendors in this wireless infrastructure management space is mFormation Technologies, Inc. Its products include an Enterprise Manager for enterprise customers and a Service Manager for wireless service providers. With Cahners In-Stat Group projecting more than 1.5 billion handsets, personal digital assistants, and Internet appliances having wireless capability by the end of 2004, companies such as mFormation are filling a critical future pain point for enterprises and for wireless service providers. While many vendors have concentrated on the wireless middleware side of the value chain, in the future the wireless infrastructure management portion of the value chain will be a critical component that should not be overlooked during enterprise deployments.

# Mobile Commerce

Mobile commerce, or m-commerce, has made several false starts over the past couple of years. Initially it was hyped along with the third-generation wireless networks (3G) and WAP in 1999 and 2000. At that time, the growth of the m-commerce market seemed just around the corner and analysts were projecting hockey-stick growth and adoption among consumers using their cell phones to make a wide range of retail purchases. As 3G rollouts were pushed back, and as user expectations fell after initial exposure to WAP-based cell phones with their user interface limitations in terms of screen size and data entry capability,  the volume of m-commerce transactions was an additional victim of the delays.

The promising signs are that m-commerce is becoming a reality almost under the radar. While consumers aren't quite buying retail products using their phones, they are starting to purchase enhancements for their phones via m-commerce transactions. Downloadable ring tones serve as one example. Today, ring tones can be purchased and downloaded to capable cell phones from a number of providers, including content companies and wireless carriers. Carrier examples include AT&T Wireless and Cingular Wireless. While ring tones appear to be a somewhat trivial service for the enterprise, they are big business for carriers and content providers targeting the teen and young adult markets. The ARC Group predicts that 551 million users worldwide will buy ring tones in 2006 and Nokia estimates it will make billions selling ring tones by the end of 2005. At a charge of $1 per ring tone or thereabouts, wireless carriers can generate revenues today and start to drive the process change to educate their consumers on making purchases for their wireless phones. Customers can often choose to pay via credit card or have the charge directly applied to their monthly bill. One of the business issues for teen-oriented trans-actions such as mobile gaming or ring tones is that teens often have prepaid cards for their cell phones. This makes billing a challenge for the wireless carrier. A solution is to provide prepaid credits for these types of m-commerce services along with the prepaid airtime credits. This is the case in Europe with the Club Nokia program. Consumers use their Club Nokia Credits, purchased via retail outlets or via their mobile phone using SMS, in order to make payments for download-ing ring tones, picture messages, operator logos, and caller group graphics. Another challenge related to ring tone downloads is that some of today's cell phones either do not support downloadable ring tones or support storage for only a limited number of downloaded ring tones on the device. As an example, the Nokia 3360 mobile phone supports up to 10 downloadable ring tones.

Mobile gaming is another m-commerce opportunity that has gained considerable attention from the wireless carriers. The wireless carriers in Europe and Asia have found that the killer applications for consumers appear to be services that are simply entertaining. One of the challenges to delivery of gaming, however, is the latency of the net-works and the current state of the art in terms of user interfaces. Gam-ing applications delivered via the network also face competition from the mobile device manufacturers such as Nokia who are placing inter-active games directly on their handsets, providing a free option for single-user games. These device manufacturer games can also be given prime placement on the device in terms of their position on the menu. Multiuser network-delivered games can generate substantial revenues for content providers and wireless operators, but an additional chal-lenge beyond the technical hurdles is the business model itself. Key questions include how the revenues are divided among the content providers and the carriers, and who provides the customer support when there are questions related to billing or content functionality.

How the mobile commerce value chain works itself out in the ring tone and mobile gaming markets is worth observation by the enterprise business audience. It may set the ground rules for who eventually owns the customer and holds the most power in the value chain. Businesses wanting to market to their customers via mobile devices will then need to work with and partner with these new incumbents in order to gain placement and priority via this channel. Key players at this point in time are clearly the wireless operators and, to some extent, the mobile device manufacturers and financial services institutions. The wireless operators own the virtual channel to the consumer through the wireless device. If they can unlock the secret to the killer applications for these devices, it is perfectly conceivable for them to migrate from providing the commoditized bandwidth and connectivity to providing the value-added data services on top of the basic pipe. Device manufacturers can appeal to consumers by enhancing and differentiating their handsets and fostering loyalty to the device and brand itself rather than to the operators' connectivity. By providing a community of interest such as Club Nokia, they can turn the devices themselves into the main offering. Finally, the financial services provider or the owner of the customers' digital wallet will certainly hold a strong position due to its level of trust and ownership of key customer information. The ability to store and manage customer contact and payment information, together with customer preferences, gives them the ability to act as an agent on the customers' behalf by screening and filtering information and transactions based on these preferences. This is a battle well worth watching for any business that sells directly to consumers.

# Location-Based Services

Location-based services promise to bring a wealth of value-added services to consumers and businesses in the form of location-specific content and applications. The technology can be applied to pinpoint the location of people or assets for tracking purposes and emergency

911 services. It can also be applied for location-relevant consumer applications such as driving directions, weather forecasts, traffic reports, concierge services, electronic marketing, electronic commerce, and other applications that can benefit from location-based personalization. In this manner, location-based services are effectively a form of personalization that takes into account the users' location. They can therefore be applied to a number of customer relationship management applications and electronic commerce applications aimed at increasing customer satisfaction and loyalty. In the supply chain, location-based services can be applied to help track goods and assets as they move throughout the supply chain from manufacturer to distributor to wholesaler and finally to retailer.

In the United States, one of the initial drivers for adoption of location-based services was the Enhanced 911 (E911) mandate from the Federal Communications Commission (FCC) in 1996. The mandate required wireless carriers to be able to locate callers to 911 emergency services with an increasing degree of accuracy over a number of phased deadlines. Phase I of the mandate required the location to be determined to a specific cell site, or cell sector, as it is known. The positional accuracy of a cell site can vary greatly due to the number of cellular towers per square kilometer and the amount of interference due to other buildings and structures between the cell sites. A cell site can generally provide an accuracy of within several hundred meters when locating a 911 caller. Phase II of the mandate, which had a deadline of October 1, 2001, was intended to provide the location of the caller within 50 to 300 meters using more elaborate positional determination than just the cell site. This mandate involved the application of either network-based or handset-based technologies in order to locate callers. The technologies available to the carriers included time difference of arrival (TDOA), angle of arrival (AOA), and RF fingerprinting for network-based solutions, and assisted GPS for handset-based solutions. Each of these solutions has strengths and weaknesses in terms of technical accuracy and cost of implementation. For example, handset-based solutions require modification to the handset and increased battery power and antenna strength. Due to the many complexities and trade-offs involved in implementing these technologies, the U.S. wireless carriers failed to meet the October 1, 2001 deadline set by the FCC. While the carriers did not meet the deadline for various reasons, the FCC mandate will still help to move the industry toward eventual adoption, with the full implementation required by the end of 2005.

Some of the vendors in the location-based services arena include Autodesk, Cell-Loc, SignalSoft, Vindigo, and Webraska. These companies have commercially available products in several markets that include both location-based services and telematics. The industry has also focused on standardization via initiatives such as the Location Inter-operability Forum (LIF), which was established by Motorola, Nokia, and Ericsson in September 2000.

Some of the barriers to adoption of location-based services include not only the cost and conversion factors being picked up by the wireless carriers but also consumer privacy issues. Consumers are rightfully concerned about how their location information will be used and who will gain access to it. This issue still has to be worked out by the industry and it is unclear who owns this information.

For the wireless operator, location-based services can help to generate additional minutes of air time and potentially fee-based transactions. For the enterprise business, the technology provides a way to deliver superior customer service. For example, tracking a delivery truck or rail car may enable a company to provide estimates for delivery time that are more accurate than general schedules and timetables. As another example, providing a customer with a location-sensitive offer from a nearby retail store can help to entice the customer to the store and generate additional revenues and brand loyalty.

When the various barriers to adoption such as privacy issues have been resolved, businesses should consider how they can add value to their customers via location-specific content and applications. For retailers with physical outlets, location-based services may be a viable technique to promote the brand and to develop deeper customer relationships. For content providers, location-based services may be a way to provide content that is more timely and personalized and therefore can demand a higher premium. The challenge will be to develop the right business model that will be convenient for customers and that will drive revenues from the marketing and sale of physical goods or digital services without impacting customer privacy.

# Telematics

While the term has several definitions, in general, telematics can be used to refer to the delivery of information and entertainment to users in their vehicles in addition to emergency services and tracking functions. Gartner Dataquest predicts that the world telematic market for combined hardware and subscription services will grow to $27 billion by 2005. Since people spend a large amount of their time in their cars, the automobile could well be the second most significant convergence platform after the home for the general consumer. By convergence platform we mean the environment where information and entertainment can be delivered via a variety of digital services offerings. Most driver interaction will probably occur via voice for safety reasons, but passengers will be able to take advantage of other forms of interaction such as touchscreen computer systems for passengers in the back of the vehicle. In the future, data connections are likely to take two forms of communication. One will be continual, or always-on, connections for emergency services and voice applications. The other will be batch-oriented, high bandwidth connections for periodic large data volume uploads of digital content to the vehicle such as digital music, videos, and navigation information.

Telematics was originally applied as an emergency services solution for luxury vehicles via the GM OnStar offering and Mercedes-Benz' Tele Aid. These services included roadside assistance, concierge services, and stolen vehicle tracking. The technology is now becoming increasingly applied toward value-added information, communications and entertainment services such as traffic information, Internet access, and email access. Some recent examples of emerging service offerings from the automotive manufacturers include Chrysler's U-Connect system, Mercedes-Benz' DriveBy InfoFueling, and various offerings from Ford, Honda, and Volvo.

>> Chrysler's U-Connect system uses a customer's existing wireless phone connection from AT&T Wireless or other providers. It uses Bluetooth technology, a short-range wireless communications protocol, in order to connect the cell phone with the vehicle's speaker system. This allows consumers to benefit from hands-free operation within their vehicles and to avoid some of the common

dual-payment issues related to purchasing multiple wireless connections for both in-car and wireless phone usage.

>> Mercedes-Benz' DriveBy InfoFueling service was demonstrated at the Comdex show in late 2001 as a research concept. It provides a broadband data stream as vehicles pass a roadside transceiver. This can help to provide data such as videos, music, and traffic reports in a batch-update scenario that does not require continuous connectivity with the vehicle.

>> Ford's Wingcast, a joint venture with Qualcomm that was formed in October 2000, has teamed up with a number of software providers such as Oracle, Sun Microsystems, KANA, and Amdocs and with Verizon Wireless to offer a complete range of telematics services and applications. The initial service will be available in certain Ford and Nissan vehicles. The company has also teamed up with Directed Electronics to offer solutions to the automotive aftermarket. One of these solutions includes Geo-Fencing, which notifies vehicle owners if their vehicle travels beyond pre-established geographic boundaries.

>> Honda is working with NTT DoCoMo in Japan to develop and bring to production a voice-driven system for email and for listening to information about local restaurants and stores.

>> Volvo's WirelessCar initiative is a joint venture with Ericsson and Telia. The venture has teamed up with Aether Systems, a wireless middleware provider, in order to provide a range of services that are independent of networks, standards, and protocols.

Along with the car manufacturers, software vendors such as Microsoft have also moved into the telematics market. Microsoft's Car.Net initiative leverages the device, channel, and platform interoperability of Web services to bring seamless content to the world of telematics. Just as Web services are helping to provide interoperability across the enterprise, they will also help to bring interoperability to the consumer world and enable end users to access content regardless of whether they are at home, in the office, or in their cars.

The challenges for the consumer telematics market will be to find the right combination of value-added services that consumers are willing to pay for beyond the basic and potentially life-saving services such as emergency roadside assistance. The best chances for widespread adoption will occur when car manufacturers begin to embed telematics in standard vehicles in addition to luxury vehicles and when creative solutions are designed to help consumers minimize the number of wireless connections they need to subscribe to. Consumers will probably be willing to pay for value-added content and services but will not want to maintain more than one or two wireless connection contracts. Ideally, their wireless services will move with them and support both mobile phone and in-car usage via creative bridging solutions such as Bluetooth.

# Electronic Tagging

Electronic tagging is a rapidly maturing technology that has tremendous potential for business applications across a wide variety of industries. Electronic tagging is part of the larger technology area of automatic identification, which includes both passive and active solutions. Automatic identification enables tags to be attached to persons or devices for automatic reading via machines. Passive tagging examples include optical, inductively coupled, capacitively coupled, and electrical techniques. The most well-known tagging solution is the optical bar code which is in widespread usage in the consumer and industrial products industry for identifying product types via universal product codes (UPC). Active tags differ from passive tags in that they contain a battery or other form of local power source. Examples include transponders and beacons that actively emit information.

One of the most interesting emerging technologies in the field of electronic tagging is the use of RFID tags, which use the inductive coupling or capacitive coupling passive techniques mentioned previously. These tags have been in use for a considerable amount of time for a variety of applications such as access control, antitheft, and asset tracking, but are now moving more squarely into the mainstream due to advances in the technology, increased standardization, and lowered prices.

RFID solutions are composed of two parts: the tag or transponder, and an electronic reader. Tags range in size and shape from that of a pencil lead or smaller, to the size of a credit card, based upon their usage requirements. The tag contains an electronic circuit that becomes operative when it is in proximity of an electronic reader. The tag then sends back a signal to the reader, providing its stored information. Tags can be read-only or read-write, allowing the information stored on the tag to be updated or replaced as dictated by business requirements related to the device or object being tracked. Tags can be read from a distance of one inch to about 100 feet or more, depending upon the power output and the radio frequency used by the reader. They can be passive or active. Active tags can be read from further distances, require less powerful readers, and can store more information, often up to one megabyte, which is just under the amount of storage on a typical floppy disk. The trade-off is that, being active, they are limited by their battery life and have increased size and cost. Battery life for active tags can still be up to 10 years.

One of the benefits of RFID solutions over other tagging solutions such as optical bar codes is that the former do not require a direct line of sight and they can function in harsh environments where bar code labels would not survive. RFID tags can actually be read through a variety of physical materials such as cardboard or plastic, in addition to being able to operate through challenging weather conditions such as rain, snow, and fog. One material they cannot penetrate, however, is metal, since the radio frequencies at which they operate are severely attenuated, or reduced in strength.

Typical RFID tags cost between $1 and $10 each, but as costs for production decline, tags will become more ubiquitous and will be attached to lower cost goods. The decreasing price point also means that they can migrate from tracking applications at the shipment or pallet level, to tracking applications at the individual package or product level. This provides greater visibility into the supply chain and can help in real-time order status and package tracking applications, in addition to helping optimize supply chain management functions such as inventory management and planning.

Some of the business applications to which tagging can be applied include access control, airline baggage identification, automotive security, document tracking, express parcel identification, livestock identification, logistics and supply chain activities, mobile commerce, product authentication, sports timing, and ticketing. Other more debated tracking applications include the tracking of parolees and also patients suffering from dementia or other diseases which may require monitoring for their own safety. While these human applications can have positive effects for the safety of the persons being tracked and the general population, they do raise privacy concerns related to these individuals being monitored 24 hours a day and having their location known at all times. The following examples show some of the current industry scenarios to which RFID tags are currently being applied:

>> Mobile Commerce—RFID tags can be applied to a variety of mobile commerce scenarios, including vending machines, retail, and customer loyalty programs. In the vending machine scenario, a customer can make a product selection from a vending machine and then pass a transponder tag past a reader embedded in the machine. The machine is then able to read the unique identification code from the tag and charge the customer's credit card account after authorizing the purchase via a host server connected to the vending machine. After the customer has been authorized to make a purchase, the vending machine is then able to dispense the selected product. An example of this scenario in action was the 2002 Winter Olympics in Salt Lake City. Texas Instruments partnered with Cola-Cola and a company called Stitch Networks to offer wireless, cashless access to vending machines at the games for 5,500 athletes, coaches, and officials.

>> Retail—In the retail space, McDonald's allows customers to use their ExxonMobil Speedpass tags for purchases either at the drive-through or within the restaurant. The Speedpass tags are simply pointed at the tag readers at the restaurant after the customer has made his or her selection and the system automatically bills the customer's credit card on file as part of his or her Speedpass profile. The benefits for the business are that transactions can be made faster, risks due to theft or incorrect payment are lowered, and customer loyalty is increased due to the convenience of the system. The SpeedPass technology from Texas Instruments was originally rolled out by Mobil Oil Corporation in 1997. It is in use at more than 3,800 ExxonMobil service stations in the United States and allows customers to pay for their gas purchases and convenience store items using their tags. The program has nearly four million users and is one of the largest RFID applications in current use. From a customer loyalty perspective, RFID tags can serve as a means to quickly identify customers as they walk into hotels, restaurants, and retail stores and allow the busi-

ness to pull up their preferences and accommodate them based upon their individual likes and dislikes.

>> Access Control—Tags can be used for access control into buildings, parking garages, and vehicles. FedEx is testing an RFID system in 200 vehicles in order to help its couriers become more productive. By using a keyless entry and ignition system for their vehicles, couriers do not have to spend time looking for keys or in using them to lock and unlock various doors to the vehicle. They are able to use a set of RFID transponders embedded into a velcro wristband, which operates when it comes within six inches of the tag readers mounted around the doors of the vehicle. The productivity gained from such as system can easily add up due to the number of deliveries made per courier and the number of couriers working for FedEx. The company operates a fleet of more than 42,500 vehicles worldwide.

>> Airline Baggage Identification—Tags can be used as part of smart labels attached to passenger luggage within the airline industry in order to provide a passenger-to-baggage verification and reconciliation solution. This type of system has received increased attention in light of the requirements of the new Aviation Transportation and Security Act which requires positive passenger bag match. The solution can benefit the airline industry by speeding the scanning process for passenger luggage. It can be done in a totally automated manner as opposed to the former bar code reading process, which required manual intervention if bags could not be read by the optical readers. British Airways first completed field trials on baggage identification back in 1999 at Heathrow Airport on behalf of the International Air Transport Association (IATA).

>> Logistics and Supply Chain—The supply chain is one of the biggest areas for productivity improvements through the application of electronic tagging. It can help facilitate real-time information management regarding the identification and location of products in all phases of the supply chain, from raw materials to manufacturing and distribution, to retail and consumers, and finally to disposal or recycling. This can help to optimize supply chain processes by reducing inventory buildups and ensuring that store shelves are full. The real-time nature of this information can help to ensure

that the forces of supply and demand across the supply chain are in constant alignment. An example is the smart pallet system in use by Unilever. The company is using TI RFID technology to manage pallet movements in their warehouse as they are loaded into various trailers. The system is able to record which pallets enter which trucks, and to verify the individual pallets' weights against the measured total weight of the truckload.

In the future, as tags become cheaper and smaller, the realm of possibilities for their application is staggering. There has recently been talk of embedding RFID tags into the fibers of Euro bank notes produced by the European Central Bank in Frankfurt, Germany. This type of application would help to prevent counterfeiting and would also fuel the mass market for RFID technology. As the Euro becomes the most widespread currency in the world, the issue of counterfeiting becomes more significant. Another benefit of placing these tags into bank notes is that it enables notes to be tracked as they move throughout the world and through a variety of hands. As bank notes are detected by a reader, their context at that moment in terms of time, location, and type of transaction activity can be added to their history in an online database. Illegal transactions would therefore be able to be tracked back to the original source of the money. One of the technical challenges of placing RFID tags into such bank notes is that they will need to be small enough and robust enough to withstand the environment and physical stress that the notes are subject to in normal usage. The price point for these tags will also need to decrease from 20 cents in order for it to be cost effective to embed them in smaller units of currency in addition to the larger 200 Euro and 500 Euro bills.

One of the goals of the Auto-ID Center at M.I.T. is to help find a mass market for the tags, which will bring their price point closer to five cents. At that price point, they become competitive for a broad number of applications and will even challenge the universal product code on printed bar code labels as the de facto standard for identifying objects. The price point for bar code labels is currently one or two cents per label.

From a size perspective, RFID chips are already in the 0.3 millimeter range in terms of height and width and are in the 60-micron range in terms of thickness. Hitachi Europe is one of the manufacturers of such chips. Additional manufacturers of RFID chips include Texas Instruments' TI*RFID division, Phillips Semiconductors, Infineon, STMicroelectronics, and Alien Technology.

In addition to the applications mentioned before, RFID tags are already finding themselves applied for solutions in the realm of science fiction. The U.S. Army has been using the tags to detect land mines by tagging bees. Since the bees are attracted to various chemical components in explosives, their movements can be traced in order to determine the proximity of land mines and other unexploded ammunition.

# Extending the Radar Lessons

>>  Along with Web services, the mobile business technologies such as wireless infrastructure management, mobile commerce, location-based services, telematics, and electronic tagging are key disruptive technologies that should be on the radar of most enterprises. They can be applied across industry in a variety of scenarios for revenue generation, performance improvement, and cost reduction.

>>  Wireless infrastructure management can help reduce costs of operation and to ensure the best possible return on investment from large-scale mobile enterprise initiatives. As more and more devices and applications are deployed to mobile workers, the enterprise needs to take more control in order to standardize the environment and to minimize support and maintenance costs.

>>  M-commerce is becoming a reality almost under the radar. While consumers aren't quite buying retail products using their phones, they are starting to purchase enhancements for their phones via m-commerce transactions. Downloadable ring tones serve as one example.

>>  Location-based services can be applied to pinpoint the location of people or assets for tracking purposes and emergency 911 services. They can also be applied for location-relevant consumer applications such as driving directions, weather forecasts, traffic reports, concierge services, electronic marketing, and electronic commerce applications.

>> The automobile could well be the second most significant con-vergence platform (the environment where information and entertainment can be delivered via a variety of digital services offerings) after the home for the general consumer, setting the stage for strong growth in telematics.

>> One of the most interesting emerging technologies in the field of electronic tagging is RFID tags. These tags have been in use for a considerable amount of time for a variety of applications such as access control, antitheft, and asset tracking, but are now moving more squarely into the mainstream due to advances in the technology, increased standardization, and lowered prices.

# Extending the Radar Considerations

>> How can wireless infrastructure management reduce costs for your management of wireless users, devices, and applications?

>> How can your business take advantage of mobile commerce in terms of sales and marketing for consumers?

>> How can location-based services be applied to improve pro-ductivity and reduce costs?

>> How can developments in telematics be applied to your busi-ness to provide new services to customers or to improve field force effectiveness?

>> How can electronic tagging such as RFID be applied within your business to reduce the bull-whip effect of the supply chain, to improve customer relationships via smartcards, or to better manage and track assets?

# Chapter

# 7

# Enterprise Security

*"You ask, what is our aim? I can answer in one word:*
*Victory – victory at all costs, victory in spite of all terror,*
*victory, however long and hard the road may be; without*
*victory, there is no survival."*

—Sir Winston Churchill

W eb services and the other technologies that have been discussed can be considered offensive technologies. They can be applied strategically as growth engines in order to capture business benefits such as increased revenues, reduced costs, and improved productivity. Security represents the other side of the equation and is equally important. It can be applied strategically as a defensive measure in order to protect the business from a variety of risks and to enable the growth engine to operate successfully. While most businesses have had security departments within their information technology groups for decades, the threat to enterprise security is becoming more severe. Attacks are becoming more diverse, more frequent, and more dangerous.

The CERT Coordination Center located at the Software Engineering Institute at Carnegie Mellon University in Pittsburgh, Pennsylvania, is one of the foremost organizations handling computer security incidents and providing analysis and statistics. It focuses on education, training, and research into survivable enterprise management and survivable network technology. Over the past decade, CERT has seen the number of reported incidents grow from 252 in 1990 to 2,412 in 1995 and to 52,658 in 2001. The vulnerabilities reported by CERT have also grown from 171 in 1995 to 2,437 in 2001. According to CERT, the possible effects of an attack include denial of service, unauthorized use or misuse of computing systems, loss, alteration, or compromise of data or software, monetary or financial loss, loss or endangerment of human life, loss of trust in the computer and network system, and loss of public confidence.

The Computer Security Institute and the FBI conducted a joint Computer Crime and Security Survey in 2001 and collected responses from over 500 U.S. corporations, government agencies, and universities. They found that 85 percent of the respondents had experienced computer security breaches within the last 12 months. Additionally, the survey found that financial losses from computer breaches had risen over the years from an average of just over $1 million per business in 2000, to an average of over $2 million per business in 2001. These data are just the tip of the iceberg, since many businesses had not quantified the extent of their financial losses or did not want to report them.

In recent years, the industry-wide costs due to security compromises have been in the billions of dollars. The "LoveLetter" virus in mid-2000 caused an estimated $6.7 billion in damages. Security compromises such as worms, which are self-propagating malicious code, have been able to cause numerous other adverse effects as well. They can spread rapidly within minutes or hours and can often cause noticeable degradation of worldwide Internet response times. As an example, the Code Red and Nimda worms infected hundreds of thousands of systems. According to CERT, the Code Red worm infected more than 250,000 systems in nine hours on July 19th, 2001. In addition to self-propagating, it was also programmed to launch a distributed denial-of-service (DDoS) attack against *www.whitehouse.gov* between the 20th and 27th days of the month. The Nimda worm caused average Internet round-trip response times to slow from around one-quarter of a second to one-half of a second on September 18th, 2001, just after it was initially detected.

The threat is that as businesses increasingly open up their networks to the outside world, they are increasingly exposing themselves to breaches in computer security. Not all threats come from the outside, and the internal employee threat is well-documented, but the increasing level of always-on connectivity to the Internet means that systems are wide open to attack and can be used as launch-pads for attacks on other systems. As we become increasingly dependent upon the Internet as a global network in order to conduct business, we are increasingly opening ourselves up to the inherent security risks of being connected. In the early days of corporate Internet adoption in the mid-1990s, security departments were horrified at the thought of connecting business applications and data to the outside world. There was a clear distinction between the internal, trusted corporate application environment and the external, untrusted environment. Somehow, along the way, the enthusiasm for "everything Internet" seemed to push these concerns aside. Today we are paying the price, with an increasing number of threats and attacks being reported. The threat is getting more severe and we are continuing to add to our level of exposure by opening holes in our networks to allow for extranets, telecommuting, and wireless access. We'll discuss wireless security later in this chapter since the topic has risen in importance due to the increasing adoption of wireless LAN technologies and the increasing adoption of wireless devices themselves.

The emerging and disruptive technologies that we have discussed earlier also add to our increasing level of vulnerability. Web services, peer-to-peer, real-time computing, and mobile business all rely on increased connectivity, sharing of resources, and rapid exchange of information in order to enable powerful business benefits. We are encoding more of our business processes and intellectual assets into software solutions and are increasingly opening these up to employees, customers, and partners. Even if the threat level stayed constant, we are substantially increasing our risks due to exposure. For these emerging technologies to be successful and to yield their promised benefits, several things must occur. Firstly, the technologies must not be oversold. Businesses must be realistic about what these enablers can and cannot do and about the level of effort required to implement them and drive changes in user behavior and adoption. Secondly, businesses need to make security an integral part of their initiatives— not just for traditional applications and processes, but for their new initiatives as well. Software vendors and service providers offering these new solutions such as Web services need to ensure that their software has the necessary security frameworks built in. They need to help educate businesses on how to implement their solutions in a secure and auditable manner.

Software vendors are now becoming more proactive about ensuring that security best practices are followed when developing their own software prior to general availability. Businesses can also help to push for greater levels of security to be built into the solutions that they utilize. For example, Microsoft's Secure Windows Initiative represents its efforts to improve the security of its server software products by educating its developers in best practices, using new tools to verify secure code, and establishing a focus on security from management. Software vendors can play a key role in addressing some of the common software vulnerabilities by shipping their products with security, in effect, "turned on" when the product is installed. Since good security policies tie back to how well software is configured in its production operation, if software is configured securely when first installed, there is a better chance of keeping these types of settings in effect. In the end, however, it is the responsibility of the business using the software to ensure that the security configurations such as authentication, access control, and encryption are properly managed and audited on an ongoing basis.

Disruptive technologies such as Web services rely on increased connectivity and sharing of resources. They also rely on the underlying movement toward software as a service and the general theme of the Internet becoming a "business operating system" for the entire universe of users, devices, and applications. Initiatives such as Microsoft's Passport and the Liberty Alliance Project founded by Sun Microsystems and others are calling upon business users and consumers to use their network-resident authentication as a universal gateway into these future applications. The concept of single sign-on authentication for a multitude of applications is highly attractive, but it will need to be adopted carefully on the part of consumers and businesses alike. As the business benefits of these disruptive technologies beckon to us, we need to understand the tradeoffs. The single sign-on services offered by the industry on this Internet business operating system are visionary, but, require considerable trust. Trust has always been one of the main barriers to adoption for businesses to leverage the Internet. Security is only one piece of the trust equation, but it is clear that security will play a key role in deciding the eventual take-up rate for these emerging solutions. The era of "build it and they will come" passed many years ago; today's era is more aptly named "trust it and they will come." It is perhaps with this in mind that Microsoft Chairman and Chief Scientist Bill Gates wrote his well-known memo to employees in early 2002 calling for a shift from focusing on software functionality to a new focus on security and privacy—something he called "trustworthy computing."

Although trustworthy computing is a superset of enterprise security, the latter can be considered the foundation upon which trust in computing can be built. The broad approach to enterprise security typically consists of three areas for consideration: prevention, detection, and reaction. This approach can be applied from the personal level all the way up to corporate and even global levels. The fight against cyberterrorism and even physical terrorism is waged in the same manner. We need to take actions to prevent it from occurring or at the very least to minimize the threat, detect when it is occurring, and be able to react swiftly to control the damage and catch the perpetrators if and when an attack does occur. In the following sections, we'll look at each of these areas and will explore some of the emerging technologies in the security arena that can be used to set up and enhance the defenses.

# Prevention

Prevention is perhaps the most powerful means of defense. We can minimize the opportunity for attacks to occur by reducing our vulnerabilities and taking aggressive approaches to control the dissemination of tools and techniques that could be used against us. Some parallels can be drawn between the preventative actions and initiatives of governments, such as the Office of Homeland Defense in the United States, and the preventative actions and initiatives that can be undertaken at the corporate level.

In the extreme case of biological, chemical, or nuclear threats, controlling the tools and techniques behind launching these types of attacks is one of the most effective ways to minimize the risk. If the tools and techniques can be secured and contained, then there are fewer individuals who would even have the knowledge or opportunity to conduct such an attack. In the case of enterprise security, it is far harder to contain the tools and techniques. Software for launching attacks on corporate systems is readily available for download on the Internet and the methods of launching an attack can be comprehended and executed by school children. It is often as simple as running a downloaded program or script. With this widespread distribution and ready availability of tools and techniques, the main recourse for corporate security specialists is to protect the boundaries. Weapons of attack are readily available or can be custom developed, so prevention measures need to move from controlling the weaponry to protecting the borders.

In the enterprise security arena, the preventative measures include software for administration, authorization, and authentication, known as 3A, firewall, and virtual private network software, secure content management software, encryption software, and vulnerability assessment software. Secure content management software primarily includes Web content, email scanning, and virus protection software that aids in securing Internet content.

The basic concept behind prevention is to protect corporate networks, applications, and data by putting up perimeter defenses, validating the identity of users, controlling access, encrypting communications, and securing applications and content. Three key ingredients are authentication, access control, and encryption. Authentication aims to validate the identity of users wanting to gain access. Traditional techniques for authentication have been the relatively weak "one-factor" user name and password approach, and the stronger "two-factor" password plus token authenticator approaches. As an example, the RSA SecurID authenticator is in use by more than 10 million people worldwide. For end users, it typically consists of a hardware key fob that generates a one-time authentication code that changes every 60 seconds. This means that users logging into a corporate network remotely need to know their password plus have the key fob in their possession. The second ingredient, access control, aims to restrict user privileges once they have been authenticated so that they have access only to the data and applications for which they have permission. It is an often tedious and time-consuming task to keep user permissions updated as new applications are added to the corporate network, but basics such as access control can go a long way toward loss prevention and risk management. The third basic security ingredient is encryption. This aims to secure content while it is resident on the internal corporate network or in transit outside the firewall. It can help to protect the integrity of data and communications so that they are not intercepted or altered in any way. Newer and more powerful encryption techniques such as the Advanced Encryption Standard (AES) and the Triple Data Encryption Standard (3DES) can be used as earlier encryption protocols such as the Data Encryption Standard (DES), first adopted by the Government in 1997, start to show signs of aging and vulnerability to cracking techniques such as brute-force attacks.

## Biometrics

Recent techniques for improved authentication include biometrics. These offerings support the recognition of a variety of human physical attributes such as voice recognition, facial recognition, fingerprinting, hand geometry, and iris recognition. The strongest form of authentication occurs when systems combine techniques in order to achieve what is known as "three-factor" authentication. This technique combines what a person knows, such as a user name and password, with what they have, such as a hardware key fob, with who they are—obtained via biometrics. However, not all security applications require this three-factor authentication or even a two-factor authentication. Facial recognition by itself can be applied to a wide variety of scenarios such as the identification of known criminals in public spaces such as airports and shopping centers, in addition to being used as part of a broader verification mechanism for high-security corporate or government applications. Some of the vendors in the facial recognition space include Viisage Technology and Visionics.

Viisage's technology was originally developed at MIT and translates facial characteristics into a unique set of numbers which they refer to as an "eigenface." Its technology can be applied for one-to-many identification processes that search large databases of millions of faces for a rapid match within seconds. It can also be applied for one-to-one verification of identity processes, such as verification at ATM machines. Viisage has the world's largest installed facial recognition database of over seven million images. Their current customers include federal government agencies, casinos, and local and state police, corrections, and social services departments.

Visionics Corporation offers a number of biometric solutions including its FingerPrinter CMS live-scan fingerprinting system and FaceIt face-recognition technology. The FingerPrinter CMS system can capture, print, and transmit fingerprints electronically to the Office of Personnel Management, where they are submitted for searching against the FBI's Integrated Automated Fingerprint Identification System database. The system can be used for a variety of background investigation purposes. For example, the Transportation and Aviation Security Act of 2001 mandated fingerprint background checks on all airport employees by the end of October 2002. A number of airports, including Los Angeles International Airport, have adopted the Visionics FingerPrinter CMS systems for this purpose. The FaceIt face recognition technology has been deployed in casinos, soccer matches, and town centers and has been used by the U.S. Army military police as part of a wearable, hands-free, facial surveillance system.

Biometrics is also starting to find more mainstream applications as well. IBM offers the FaceIt face recognition software when customers purchase their UltraPort Camera for ThinkPad A, T, or X Series laptops. The software is part of a screensaver that can restore access to the laptop when the authorized face appears in view of the camera.

## Wireless Security

With the proliferation of wireless devices and wireless access points such as wireless LANs, the opportunity to get onto a private network has never been higher. Instead of being protected behind physical security such as buildings, locked doors, and guards, corporate networks with wireless access are now, in effect, floating freely up and down office floors and even outside buildings. Wireless LANs are a particular problem because they spread the data signal in an uncontrolled dispersion pattern to anyone within the signal radius wanting to tap into the network. This dispersion can often be 500 to 1,000 feet. On an unsecured wireless LAN, all that is required to gain access to the network is a laptop with a wireless modem attached. A number of hardware and software vendors are on hand, however, to provide solutions. These solutions are similar to the wired network solutions and aim to offer firewalls, virtual private networks, and other forms of access control, authentication, and encryption for wireless data and devices. An example is the VPN-1 SecureClient from Check Point Software Technologies. The software provides virtual private network and firewall functionality for PDA devices such as the Compaq iPaq. In this way it provides mobile device users with the same type of protection that they have when using their laptops. The firewall serves as protection for the mobile device from attack and the VPN serves to ensure secure communications with the corporate network. Novartis, an international pharmaceutical company, is using the Check Point software to secure network access via Pocket PC devices for over 10,000 of their remote employees. For a long time, security has been one of the major barriers to adoption for mobile computing beyond niche, specialized applications. These types of security solutions for mobile devices will aid in the overall growth and acceptance of wireless computing as a whole, in addition to protecting wireless communications and the devices themselves.

With mobile devices such as cell phones and PDAs gaining more and more functionality, it is becoming critical for businesses to secure their devices to the same level as their desktop computing infrastructure. Wireless and mobile devices are gaining more processing power, more storage, and more access to business applications such as corporate email, personal information management, and sales and field force applications. They are also gaining business intelligence functions as corporations summarize business events and key performance indicators into digital dashboards for constant reporting and notification purposes. This type of information, if compromised, can be a significant risk for most businesses across a number of industries. It may include financial data, sales information, customer lists, competitive information, operational data, and other sensitive corporate metrics. Loss of a wireless device such as a PDA will shortly be as serious an issue as the loss of a regular laptop. Without the proper protection, these devices will be easy prey for individuals wanting to steal sensitive information or to gain access into your network. One of the steps to secure mobile computing is to standardize which types of devices are permitted onto the corporate network and to establish sound authentication, access control, and encryption policies and procedures.

# Detection

Detection of security breaches can often be a challenge due to the complexity of today's computing environments. Businesses often do not understand the full scope of the normal working interactions of their own applications and processes, let alone the patterns of network activity or changes to data that may signal an attack. Detection involves being able to know when an attack is in progress and being able to separate real attacks from innocent, but unusual, behavior on the network. Defining what constitutes unusual behavior is part of the problem, since breaches can originate from a variety of sources, can be aimed at a variety of targets, and, have a variety of motivations behind them. Attacks can also vary widely depending upon the class of attack and can be conducted over short or long durations of time. An attack may not be apparent until a certain pattern of behavior has been observed for hours or even days.

As a best practice, detection must minimize the number of false positives. Too many false positives can lead to intrusion alerts that are taken less seriously and are reacted to with less urgency. Rather than being a standalone tactic, detection should be part of an overall security strategy and approach. Security policies should firstly define the levels of security that are required for various assets. Certain data, applications, and network elements will need to be more secure than others. Detection systems should first be applied to protect the most critical infrastructure elements within the organization. Security policies should also document best practices for network, application, and data configuration. Detection systems should look for both incoming network attacks via network monitoring and for changes to data such as Web pages or sensitive documents via host-based monitoring. For this reason, intrusion detection systems often fall into these two categories and include a central management function that can provide a single, centralized console for monitoring both data and network integrity status.

When making a decision related to the detection of security breaches, businesses can choose either to keep the function in-house or to outsource the function to a managed security services provider, or MSSP. MSSPs typically offer both intrusion detection systems

(IDSs) and antivirus services as a part of their service offering. They also typically provide firewall, virtual private network, and vulnerability assessment services. For small- and medium-sized businesses, MSSPs can present an attractive way to gain these types of services at a lower total cost of ownership than by building the competency themselves. Larger enterprises are also starting to adopt MSSPs despite their initial apprehension about the outsourced business model and the stability of vendors. Most large enterprises favor keeping security in-house in order to maintain stricter control and not to rely on third parties for such a critical part of their business. The truth is, however, that many MSSPs are improving their value proposition for the business by providing well-defined service level agreements and by building their reputations for delivering quality customer service, best practices, and responsiveness.

## Intrusion Detection

Intrusion detection software provides an alert mechanism for security breaches but can also help to protect data and network integrity in real time. For example, the Tripwire for Web Pages technology from Tripwire can detect changes to Web page content and can prevent changed content from being served to end users. Instead, it replaces the altered pages with a customized message that states that the page is temporarily unavailable. This can help to minimize public incidents due to "cyberhooliganism," financial losses, and downtime for problem resolution. In this manner, it maintains Web site integrity in addition to performing the real-time notification function. The company makes several intrusion detection products that can be applied to servers and also to a variety of infrastructure elements such as routers and switches that help to direct the flow of Internet traffic.

One of the first questions when deploying intrusion detection systems is where to place them on the corporate network. The National Security Agency recommends that intrusion detection sensors be located at positions on the network based upon the number of sensors available and the determination of what is critical infrastructure. It recommends that the first sensor be placed in the demilitarized zone, known as the DMZ, between the router and firewall, in order to protect from incoming attacks from the Internet. The second recommended location is on the corporate intranet just behind the firewall.

This can help to detect attacks that have successfully breached the initial line of defense. Finally, it recommends that additional intrusion detection sensors be placed on critical local area network points within the Intranet, and on critical servers such as file servers, Web servers, and mail servers. The takeaway here is that intrusion detection needs to be placed along critical points of the infrastructure with a layered approach.

# Reaction

While a variety of preventative measures can be employed in order to minimize the risk of attack, no business or organization can be completely safe. No matter how much is invested in security, there will always be vulnerabilities that can be exploited either purposefully or accidentally. While increased investment can close the most apparent vulnerabilities, there is a law of diminishing returns. There is no investment amount that can guarantee absolute security. The challenge is in determining the right amount of investment that is required in order to reduce the possibility of attacks to an acceptable level from a risk-management perspective. As security measures are scaled up, there is an ease-of-use cost to pay in addition to a financial cost. End users within a business like to have easy access to their applications and data and often complain if security measures become what is seen as too much of an obstacle. In this respect, an education process is necessary. End users may need to sacrifice some convenience to keep their applications and data more secure and more resilient from corruption, either intentionally or unintentionally. Education can help them better understand the importance of both physical and computer-based security and the consequences when this is incorrectly applied or omitted.

The good news is that alternative techniques that allow increased computing security with improved ease of use for end users are becoming available. These techniques include a number of authentication mechanisms such as handwriting recognition, facial recognition, smartcards, and image-based passwords as opposed to character-based passwords. Image-based passwords use a person's ability to remember visual patterns instead of strings of characters. Since most people choose very obvious text-based characters that can easily be cracked by publicly available software, the image-based password approach can aid in making authentication more effective and easier to use at the same time. However, each technique has its advantages and disadvantages, so authentication techniques need to be evaluated on a case-by-case basis. These cost and ease-of-use factors typically limit the level of security measures that can be put into place by a typical business. Education can play a strong role, but most businesses will never get close to having absolute security due to these financial and acceptance issues.

Breaches to security can occur in a variety of situations that are often unrelated to deliberate attacks. Even poorly tested or configured software can be a major issue and source of vulnerability. Since Web applications are, for the most part, stateless, information about the current users and their current activity often has to be passed along from one Web page to the next in order to maintain the users' "session." This session is their context of activity and, in e-commerce scenarios, is thought of as their electronic shopping cart. Often, the users' session is maintained by passing codes in the request to the next Web page and is visible to end users as extra characters on the address line within the browser. If this address line is left unencrypted, curious end users can experiment with these codes and can pull up other people's information by changing the values within the codes. This is a very simple example of a vulnerability, but one that occurs frequently. If this happens to a financial institution and the matter gets reported to the media, it can be a major incident that is costly in terms of customer and shareholder relations. It is therefore important to ensure that security best practices are put into place not only within the runtime computing environment, but also in the development environment. Business analysts and developers need to think about security from the requirements and design stage onward. Too often, security is considered as an afterthought after bugs have been found or after breaches have occurred. The software problem extends to poorly configured or poorly updated security policies and patches as well. The fact is that fixes to vulnerabilities are often readily available before the attacks. Businesses need to ensure that access policies are maintained and that the most recent patches are installed on their systems. Without ongoing updates, a system is open to exposure on a daily basis.

When computer security breaches do occur, a response plan can be used to minimize the damage. These types of responses can be prepared at the business level, the industry level, or even at the national or global level. For example, the G7 has prepared joint exercises in order to test the international level response to biological, chemical, or nuclear terrorist attacks. Whether it is at the international level or the corporate level, responses are most effective when there is a clear plan in place. A plan should incorporate people, process, and technology. It should be clear who needs to be involved, which outside parties such as law enforcement need to be contacted, when they need to be contacted, and what steps can be taken to immediately counter the attack and to minimize the damage. Depending upon the level of attack, damage control can be both an IT exercise and a business and public relations exercise. Since notice of an attack in progress or of a severe vulnerability may come from a variety of sources, response plans need to incorporate the appropriate steps to be taken by all user constituencies who could first gain notice of a problem. Customer support staff must be aware of how to handle incoming calls from customers who may first discover an issue and know who to contact for the next level of support.

In addition to closing the vulnerability, businesses need to be aware of how they should document and track an attack in progress or one that has recently taken place. Accurate human and computer-based logging, event tracking, reporting, and documentation of the nature and sequence of the occurrences can help identify the perpetrators or the originating systems. One of the problems today is that attacks often come from innocent servers that have been compromised by malicious software themselves. These types of attacks are usually blocked by the firewall, however, which can intercept an incoming attempt to access a machine or communications port on the network. A well-prepared and well-rehearsed incident response plan can help minimize the damage caused by attacks. During an attack is no time to be determining who to call for help, and if they are outside security specialists, it is no time to be determining the rules of engagement. Security specialists need to be able to perform their tasks and have ready access to applications and data as required. Upfront planning is therefore critical to business continuity and disaster recovery efforts.

# Estimating Results

Security has historically been hard to quantify in terms of its return on investment. Expected returns are usually based on the principle that the costs of not implementing security can far outweigh the costs of implementing it. We know that the costs of not implementing security can be devastating for those businesses that are subject to attacks, carelessness, or even simply bad luck. The costs can impact business operations, revenues, customer relationships, shareholder value, and even business life expectancy. These devastating effects can also occur within minutes, hours, or days.

The challenge has always been how to determine how much security is adequate. The law of diminishing returns and the unpredictability of the nature and timing of attacks means that no investment amount is ever enough to offer complete security. An organization must determine its own risk profile and the amount of risk it can tolerate.

Some of the suggested solutions can be on the higher end of security costs since they are newer, more powerful enablers for protection, detection, and reaction. Investing in security requires more planning than most packaged business application investments. For those business applications, all that is required is an implementation plan and solid program and project management. In the security arena, technologies need to be selected and implemented, but that is only part of the solution. A continual program of education, management, and monitoring is required. Security policies and procedures have to be living documents that are frequently updated to reflect changes in the nature of threats and vulnerabilities and in changes to the direction of the business. A constant vigilance has to be in effect and defenses need to be updated in real time with the latest patches and fixes. If all goes well, nothing happens. If things do not go well, nothing good happens.

A return on investment formula for security can take the cost of implementing security measures versus the costs due to losses if the measures are not in place. Costs due to losses can be measured in a variety of ways. They can include lost revenues, for example, from an online storefront, and costs for bringing the business back online and restoring systems and data to their original state prior to any corruption. In extreme circumstances, costs can also include the larger-impact, but more intangible, costs of lost customer confidence, lost customers, and reduced stock price.

A total return-on-investment formula can also include the cost savings in IT management of security that can be gained by moving toward centralized management and applications such as single sign-on. Single sign-on increases productivity by allowing end users to authenticate themselves once to gain access to a number of enterprise applications. These types of centrally managed applications and end-user convenience factors can make employees more productive even as users, devices, and applications proliferate. Without it, increased levels of security can be a drain on productivity rather than an enabler.

A basic return-on-investment formula for security is as follows:

*Return on security investment = Tangibles + Intangibles =*
*(Minimized business disruption + Increased IT*
*productivity) / (IT costs) + Increased business resiliency*

Investments in security can provide strong returns on investment from cost avoidance. The amount of cost avoidance is hard to predict, but increasing availability of industry statistics can help to profile the most common classes of attack and the costs that they can incur. As private industry and the Government align more closely to protect critical infrastructure after the terrorist attacks of 2001, there is hope that more data on security breaches will be shared. This sharing of data will help to build a more accurate profile of the costs associated with attacks and of the nature and frequency of attacks experienced by the business community. As we learn more about the types of threats and vulnerabilities, we can focus resources in the right areas with the right technologies and processes in order to prevent, detect, and react. By doing so, we can then refocus the business on the offensive, using emerging technology as a growth engine, secure in the knowledge that the defenses are squarely in place.

# Extending the Radar Lessons

>> As we become increasingly dependent upon the Internet as a global network in order to conduct business, we are increasingly opening ourselves up to the inherent security risks of being connected.

>> Emerging and disruptive technologies add to our increasing level of vulnerability. We are encoding more of our business processes and intellectual assets into software solutions and are increasingly opening these up to employees, customers, and partners. Even if the threat level stayed constant, we are increasing our risks due to exposure substantially.

>> The basic concept behind prevention is to protect corporate networks, applications, and data by putting up perimeter defenses, validating the identity of users, controlling access, encrypting communications, and securing applications and content.

>> The strongest form of authentication occurs when systems combine techniques in order to achieve "three-factor" authentication. This technique combines what a person knows, such as a user name and password, with what he or she has, such as a hardware key fob, with who he or she is—obtained via biometrics.

>> With mobile devices such as cell phones and PDAs gaining ever more functionality, it is critical for businesses to secure their devices to the same level as their wired computing infrastructure.

>> Businesses often do not understand the full scope of the normal working interactions of their own applications and processes, let alone the patterns of network activity or changes to data that may signal an attack. Intrusion detection software provides an alert mechanism for security breaches and can also help to protect data and network integrity in real time.

>> A well-prepared and well-rehearsed incident response plan can help minimize the damage caused by attacks. During an attack is no time to be determining who to call for help. Upfront planning is critical to business continuity and disaster recovery efforts.

> *Return on security investment = Tangibles + Intangibles*
> *= (Minimized business disruption + Increased IT*
> *productivity) / (IT costs) + Increased business resiliency*

# Extending the Radar Considerations

>> How well-prepared is your business in terms of preventing, detecting, and reacting to security breaches, either deliberate or accidental?

>> Has your corporate security scaled up in order to meet the challenges of increased connectivity, increased access, and increased threats?

>> Will you know when you are being attacked, and do you have a well-rehearsed incident response plan?

>> What is your organization's return on security investment and your tolerance for business disruption?

>> Do you have the correct balance of offensive and defensive technologies to both grow your business and to protect your business?

# 8

# Emerging Technology Strategic Roadmap

*"Perception is strong and sight weak. In strategy it is impor-
tant to see distant things as if they were close and to take a
distanced view of close things."*

—Miyamoto Musashi

Having outlined many emerging and disruptive technologies that could well be on your radar as future solutions,
it's time to discuss an approach that the enterprise can
take in order to best leverage these technologies and extract business
value. A formalized process will help to keep the radar in motion and
to institutionalize the process for moving enabling technologies from
theory into practice and into solid business benefits. It forms an
action plan or strategic roadmap for continuous radar operations—
detecting and responding with intelligence in terms of understanding
the threats and opportunities and applying the best resources at the
best leverage points. Radar makes an excellent analogy. It provides an
early warning system for events on the horizon, giving the enterprise
time to craft a strategic response and to either put up defenses or to
launch a counterattack.

The term radar is an acronym for RAdio Detection And Ranging.
Applied to the enterprise, a comparison can be drawn in terms of
detecting emerging technologies and determining the timing of their

impact in terms of when they should be leveraged. Additionally, conventional radars have to deal with background noise and have their threshold set to indicate legitimate targets whose signal is above the ambient noise level. The signal-to-noise ratio measures the strength of the true signal when compared to the background noise. A good signal-to-noise ratio means that targets can readily be identified. If the signal-to-noise ratio approaches the number "one" or lower, then it is often hard to discern true targets from false alarms due to background noise. A similar issue applies to the enterprise when implementing an emerging technology radar. The technology hype cycle can boost the noise levels for new technologies, leading to overinflated expectations and, in effect, false alarms or at least alarms that are too early to be effectively acted upon.

Continuing the analogy, a conventional radar is comprised of seven basic components: a power supply, synchronizer, display, transmitter, receiver, duplexer switch, and antenna. For the enterprise, the power supply relates to funding and executive buy-in. It drives the entire device. The synchronizer relates to the timing and frequency of radar activities, i.e., how often the signal is sent out and how often it is interpreted. The transmitter, receiver, and duplexer relate to the information-gathering processes, i.e. collaborative discussions for information acquisition via internal and external sources. The antenna relates to the strategic direction in which the technology radar is pointed, i.e., knowing which software categories to focus on and to listen for. Finally, the display relates to the actionable information and work products that are the output of the entire radar process for business leaders to react to and refine their business strategies. Figure 8-1 shows this radar analogy in terms of these seven basic components. The enterprise equivalent is shown in the parentheses below each component.

The basic steps for setting this emerging technology direction are to establish the radar process, to understand how to operate the radar, to prioritize detected events, to take appropriate actions, and to constantly monitor results. Translating this approach for the enterprise yields several action items. Even if you have some form of radar already in place, it's worth continually monitoring its performance and tuning as necessary. Particular emphasis should be placed on extending the radar to look out further for emerging and disruptive technologies.

**Figure 8-1** Basic Components in Radar Analogy for Emerging and Disruptive Technologies. Source: Adapted from Federation of American Scientists, Military Analysis Network.

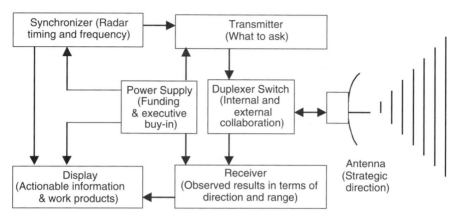

Venture capitalists, software companies, and high-tech companies tend to have well-tuned radars since it is part of their business to be ahead of the curve. Budgets for research and development can be extremely high in the software and high-tech sector since keeping ahead of the competition is the only way to ensure survival. For example, according to the MIT Technology Review's Corporate R&D Scorecard 2001, spending on R&D as a percentage of revenue for the software sector ranged from 10 to nearly 30 percent for some of the highest ranked R&D spenders, including Microsoft, Oracle, and SAP. Microsoft's R&D budget was close to $4 billion during that period. In terms of percentage of revenues, I2 and Electronic Arts were both close to 30 percent. Turning to the typical enterprise, even though companies invest heavily in R&D, they may not have a radar process in place to help detect enterprise software innovations that can be strategic to their business. Any existing radar process for detecting new enterprise software innovations may well be just a part-time, informal activity for several executives and not currently a formalized process. A lot of the traditional R&D budget is focused on developing new products, such as new semiconductor products and new pharmaceuticals, and bringing them to market, but not on bringing outside technologies into the enterprise to improve business operations. Additionally, as revenues show slower growth rates or even decline, many enterprises face cuts to their R&D budgets. R&D often needs to produce more innovation from less investment.

As the rest of the economy becomes ever more virtualized and increasingly starts to expose its business functions as software services over the next several years, the need for advanced radar systems specific to these areas increases substantially. The enterprises' products in terms of value creation will increasingly become manifested as software. Therefore more R&D budget needs to be directed toward virtual products as well as physical products and services. A manufacturing company may have physical products and a large R&D budget dedicated to bringing new products to market, but the war in terms of competitive advantage will be increasingly fought on the battlefield of business agility driven by software applications and processes.

Within the IT department, with more and more capital expenditure of the enterprise moving into information technology, a well-tuned radar can help to ensure that every dollar invested is focused on the right technologies for each business objective. It can also help to detect emerging technologies that can perform similar business functions as older technologies for less cost, in terms of development and ongoing maintenance, or to provide greater and more flexible output in terms of enterprise value for the same cost as the older technologies.

# Action Items for Extending the Radar

With the case for extending the radar now established, here are some action items that you can take within your enterprise in order to create, extend, and operate your radar. The radar should cross the divide between business and technology and feed into the overall business strategy of the organization. It is a radar that should interoperate alongside other radars tuned to detecting customer satisfaction and loyalty, employee feedback, partner feedback, competitive intelligence, and general market dynamics.

### Action Item #1: Set clear objectives and ensure buy-in for the emerging technology radar process

In creating the radar process for emerging and disruptive technologies within your enterprise, the first step is to ensure that you have executive buy-in. Executives need to understand that this process is critical for ongoing competitive advantage and even for long-term survival. Although economic pressures may push for an operational focus on sales and delivery of products and services, ignoring the radar process can place future revenues in jeopardy, slow down innovation, and can lead to missed opportunities for cost reduction and improvements in productivity, entry into new markets, and customer loyalty. It can also affect your customers' perception of your business as an innovator.

The resources allocated to the radar process can certainly vary based upon economic conditions, but the radar must be activated and be continuous in its operation. To ensure buy-in, look for prior successes and rapid techniques to deliver value. Be sure to promote success stories where your radar has detected critical technologies and has turned them into business benefits. Even the detection process can be valuable to executives. Knowing what is being picked up on the radar can show useful trends and help to steer the ship. Monthly or weekly reports to executives can give them a snapshot of current trends and impacts for their business and for the business of their customers and business partners. This can also enable cross-sell and up-sell opportunities on top of existing business.

To ensure executive buy-in, it is important to make certain that the radar is described in the correct manner. Rather than a purely technology radar, which can often be viewed as a "science fair" or experiment, it should be described as a process to detect emerging and disruptive technologies that have a strategic impact on the business. The articulation of business impact is critical here. Executives will need the translation from technical innovations to business impact. Only by conveying the business impact of these technologies will you be able to ensure buy-in for the process itself. In this regard, the translation from technical innovation to business impact should be made immediately upon detection, and the technical details should be held as background or supplementary information only.

## Action Item #2: Put a business process in place to extend your current radar

Once the objectives for the radar have been set and there is buy-in from executives, you can create a business process to operate the radar. The business process can have steps and gates from one step to the next as the highest potential initiatives move through the process and others are rejected. The entire process can also dovetail in with downstream IT strategy, corporate strategy, and business development activities.

The first step in the process is the detection phase. Detection should be allowed to come from both internal and external sources. Look for ways to involve external advisors such as customers, business partners, consultants, software companies, academics, venture capitalists, analysts, and the media. The detection mechanism should include a network of trusted business advisors. Customer and business partner representation can help to ensure that the various insights and possible directions are oriented back toward the main business focus of serving the customer. In this regard, customers should often be at least 50 percent of the overall advisory board, if not more.

The benefits of a formal radar process include reduced duplication of effort, improved communications across business units and geographies, reduction of missed opportunities, early detection of key enabling technologies, and improved reuse of emerging technology throughout the organization. The business processes behind radar operation should be continually refined as you learn what output work products are most effective and which processes are most effective. A streamlined, lightweight approach is often the best starting point in order to take a quick scan of the landscape. Having multiple targets on the radar will help to ensure that the process is kept simple and efficient and that the output work products begin to take shape.

## Action Item #3: Prioritize emerging and disruptive technologies in the context of your business objectives

Once the radar process has been put into action and is detecting enabling technologies, the next phase is to prioritize these opportunities based upon business impact. The final prioritization should be performed by a representative group of executives from various business units across the company, but the initial scoring can be made by one or more individuals in order to capture the first impressions. Current business objectives should be used as the lens by which opportunities are judged. A simple grading mechanism can help convey initial grades to the group for feedback and final adjustment. It is often typical to have two categories of grades, one for the general technology or solution area under investigation, such as Web services or real-time computing, and another grade at a more granular level aimed at certain initiatives or certain vendor solutions within one of the general technology categories.

It may well be that a certain vendor solution is scored highly but that the technology area is scored lower due to its emerging, immature nature and certain internal or external business hurdles that may need to be overcome prior to adoption. The timing of market entry is an important factor. Enter too early and the business may get caught up in a higher degree of risk due to incomplete standards, unreliable vendor products, or lack of industry-wide acceptance of a particular solution. Enter too late and the competitive advantage may be lost.

With the top initiatives graded, these technology areas and particular initiatives and vendors can be monitored on an ongoing basis. Those that show the most potential can be moved through the gate to the next process step. This is probably the formation of a business case around the opportunity or development of a proof-of-concept. Those solutions that are seen as attractive, but still immature, can be placed on hold for continued observation until the timing of market entry or adoption is more favorable.

## Action Item #4: Look for ways to embed emerging and disruptive technologies into current initiatives

Not all of these emerging technologies form standalone solutions to enterprise challenges. As we saw in Chapter 1, many of these technologies form a new infrastructure layer that should be embedded into existing initiatives as well as be leveraged for entirely new solutions. Thus, when prioritizing these technologies, be sure to look for cost takeout opportunities and opportunities to enhance business value in current initiatives in addition to the creation of solutions to new business problems. This is important because being able to extract more value from existing investments is a key priority and can often be accomplished more rapidly than new product development or new implementation. Being able to rejuvenate existing software assets extends their longevity and thus their return on investment.

For example, one simple way to adopt Web services is to start by applying the technology for cost savings in the software development lifecycle and for enterprise application integration initiatives. Not only will this provide cost takeout from IT expenditures, it will also create a greater range of future options in the solutions that are developed or integrated due to the flexibility of software when implemented in the Web services paradigm. Web services can be applied as a wrapper around existing technology assets such as mainframes and other legacy systems. In this manner, the business can benefit from improved access to legacy data and applications without requiring a rewrite of the core business logic embedded within these applications.

As another example, wireless and mobile technologies can either be leveraged in a standalone manner for a specific enterprise function or they can be applied to enhance existing solutions as an additional channel. A standalone solution example might be a complete field force automation application delivered via PDA for workers in the utility industry. Field force automation is a prime candidate for mobile enablement since it often has a number of process inefficiencies that mobile automation can help to streamline. An embedded solution example might be the availability of order status lookup via cell phone, pager, or PDA for business customers of a major chemicals manufacturer. By enhancing the existing solution of desktop browser-based order status lookups, the emerging technology is applied to enhance an existing business process by opening up a new communications channel and level of convenience for the business customers.

Thus, in addition to applying these technologies for new solutions, be certain to apply them for enhancing existing solutions and as a strategic upgrade for your business operations and enterprise IT systems and processes. On the IT side, this upgrade can include application development, deployment and management techniques, enterprise IT architecture, best practices and standards, and enterprise security. On the business side, the upgrade can be applied to almost any existing initiatives that have business processes transacted via software.

## Action Item #5: Combine emerging and disruptive technologies holistically

The new waves of emerging technologies are highly synergistic with one another. Many of them are enabling technologies that apply at the infrastructure level as fundamental building blocks for business applications to be constructed upon. The much sought-after "killer application" is probably not a single application or a single technology enabler such as Web services or RFID, but a holistic combination of enablers. Just as silos have historically been created in Internet, intranet and extranet applications, or in various packaged applications, silos can just as easily be created from emerging technology. The challenge for the business is to unlock the right combinations of these enabling technologies that will yield the maximum business benefit.

A holistic approach that views these enablers in terms of their potential impact and value for employees, customers, and suppliers will yield the best results. As an example, Web services and peer services can be applied both internally and externally. Mobile business can likewise be applied for employee productivity or for improved customer and supplier interaction and responsiveness. When wireless applications are combined with real-time computing initiatives, location-based services, and RFID technologies, the business possibilities and the range of opportunities become far greater. One of the key questions to ask is how business objectives such as increased agility and productivity can be generated by the addition of these technologies. How can greater value be extracted by making information and transactions more fluid? How can the intelligence and reaction time of the business be improved by moving to more interoperable, real-time, resource-efficient, flexible, and secure systems? Be aware, however, that these enablers are not a magic bullet. There may still be considerable heavy lifting to be done in terms of application development, integration, and process change. The good news is that the tools for performing the work are improving and the newly constructed artifact will have vastly improved capabilities from the previous generation of e-business applications.

One of the legacies of the e-business explosion in the late 1990s was the large increase in the number of categories of enterprise software and an even bigger increase in the number of software companies. There is now an alphabet soup of acronyms that describe different categories of software solution from which to choose. One result of this wide array of new categories is that enterprise decision makers often consider each one in a vacuum. A business may embark on a Web services initiative, a peer-to-peer initiative, or a mobile business initiative and see them as wholly separate ventures.

By looking at the broader context of these technologies, their characteristics, and how they can be exploited, businesses can find ways to combine initiatives and achieve synergies. The challenge for the innovative enterprise is to look beyond individual software categories, as defined by the software companies or the analysts, and apply them in combination to respond to business challenges.

The following three scenarios may help to illustrate how the technologies can be combined:

>> A human resources department decides to cut costs by automating enrollment procedures for medical, dental, and eye-care plans. To achieve this, it uses Web services software to aggregate services from various benefit providers and create a common interface for staff; business process management techniques to help design and execute the required business processes for each provider during enrollment; and peer services, for person-to-person communication, to enable IT departments to collaborate during implementation of the system and to help benefits departments service employees afterwards.

>> A manufacturing equipment vendor incorporates an embedded system in its customers' machinery. The system continuously transmits performance information to the vendor's headquarters; when a potential fault is detected, the vendor sends a message to a field service worker's smartphone or PDA, prompting the worker to inspect the equipment. The vendor can thus fix potential equipment problems before they disrupt its customers' business.

>> Within the supply chain, information on the quality of goods received at a warehouse is recorded on a PDA with wireless connectivity. The results are transmitted to a real-time system, cou-

pled with Web services integration to partner systems, in order to manage vendor quality. The real-time nature of the information flow helps reduce cycle times and increase productivity compared with more traditional batch-orientated processes. Information captured electronically at the point of activity also eliminates the need for duplicate data entry in the back office, hence improving data accuracy.

Over the past decade, the technical challenge for businesses has been to implement large packaged software applications such as enterprise resource planning, customer relationship management, and supply chain management systems. The challenge over the next decade will be to implement the next generation of software in a manner that is category-agnostic. In other words, how enterprises exploit the business and technical linkages and overlaps between software categories and components will be more critical than the functions of the components themselves. As enterprises become more virtual and more business functions are outsourced, the raw elements of speed and flexibility and the level of collaboration between software components will be key factors in creating a competitive advantage.

To exploit all these technologies fully, the business must take a holistic view and be prepared to incorporate as many technologies as are required by its objectives. The lesson from the e-business era is that even emerging technologies can create silos of functionality within a business. Just as Internet, intranet, and extranet functional silos were combined several years ago, so the next generation of information technology advances should be combined during the planning stage rather than as an afterthought. This approach will help maximize the achievement of business objectives and minimize the number of islands of automation. One of the challenges will be that the holistic view will probably cross several vendor products. Making these products all work together will be an integration challenge, but one that will create higher levels of competitive advantage rather than simply implementing prepackaged solutions.

When taking the holistic approach, it is also important to look not just at software innovations but also at developments in the hardware and networking side as well. Chapter 9, describes some of the new innovations in this space, including grid computing, computing on demand, personal mobile gateways, and fuel cells.

If we look at the core attributes of these seemingly disparate software categories discussed in the previous chapters, we find that they are, in fact, intricately related. The technologies deal with advances in machine-to-machine integration and standardization, person-to-person collaboration, the speed of information flow, flexibility of process, and mobility. All these characteristics need to be embedded in the next generation of business processes, transactions, and interactions as fundamental building blocks for a new business architecture. What's promising is that these advances also indicate that we are starting to shape technology around ourselves and our business processes instead of shaping ourselves around technology. The new business architecture brought about by this new wave of enabling technologies will help to create a digital business operating system that can enable both time-based and capabilities-based competitive advantage.

## Action Item #6: Apply emerging technologies to operate the radar itself

Emerging technologies can be applied to operate the radar itself. In addition to the typical use of electronic spreadsheets and documents, a collaborative hub can be used to serve as an ongoing knowledge base accessible by both internal executives and external advisors. As corporations increasingly focus on external as well as internal inputs for detecting emerging trends, an enterprise portal can help serve as a hub for the knowledge management and collaborative aspects of the radar process. For example, information and documents from outside advisors can be posted on the portal and competitive intelligence documents can also be uploaded.

There are several opportunities available when looking to emerging technologies to help operate the radar. Peer services, or peer-to-peer, can be applied for the collaborative aspects of the knowledge portal for functions such as instant messaging, chat rooms and whiteboards. Web services can be applied in order to automate the integration of data feeds from news sites and to capture competitive intelligence in real time. Business process management tools can be applied to help manage the process of moving detected technologies from theory to practice with the relevant approval steps and workflow among decision makers. Mobile business technologies can be applied to serve as an executive dashboard into the radar, highlighting key metrics and information.

Using emerging technologies to operate the radar has another advantage as well. It can help to evangelize these new techniques and serve as a valuable demonstration of their capabilities. Many of the executives who are exposed to the internal radar operation in terms of decision making on future investments may have limited time to explore the actual details picked up by the radar. Having material presented to them using the most promising technologies under investigation can help to put some of the theory into practice.

## Action Item #7: Continually monitor and adjust your emerging technology radar process

The final action item is to ensure that the radar is kept in constant operation and is continually adjusted. It is important to set up the network of input sources from both IT staff and business executives. New solutions may come to light from either of these sources and monitoring both business and IT developments can help to ensure that the radar is scanning all areas of opportunity.

Analyst reports and predictions for emerging technologies can help to indicate certain possibilities, but they must then be filtered for your specific business needs and industry segment in order to gauge applicability. Requirements driven by customers and business partners are even better since they will help to drive development of the right strategic capabilities. Once the radar process is in place, one of the benefits is that its operation can be scaled up or down, in terms of investment and level of ongoing effort, as needed, based upon business constraints. Continual monitoring and adjustment of the radar process become a small percentage of the effort once the initial process and procedures have been defined.

# Extending the Radar Lessons

Action Items for extending the radar

>> Action Item #1: Set clear objectives and ensure buy-in for the emerging technology radar process.

>> Action Item #2: Put a business process in place to extend your current radar.

>> Action Item #3: Prioritize emerging and disruptive technologies in the context of your business objectives.

>> Action Item #4: Look for ways to embed emerging and disruptive technologies into current initiatives.

>> Action Item #5: Combine emerging and disruptive technologies holistically.

>> Action Item #6: Apply emerging technologies to operate the radar itself.

>> Action Item #7: Continually monitor and adjust the emerging technology radar process.

# Extending the Radar Considerations

>> Does your business have an emerging technology radar process?

>> How can you maximize executive buy-in?

>> How critical is the emerging technology radar process for your organization's future and business objectives?

>> What technologies need to be on the radar today and how can they be translated into business value?

>> How can you most effectively turn radar detection events into competitive advantage?

# Chapter

# 9

# Future Trends

*"I am a HAL Nine Thousand computer, Production Number 3. I became operational at the HAL Plant in Urbana, Illinois, on January 12, 1997."*

—*2001: A Space Odyssey*

A number of computing initiatives currently underway provide a glimpse of some of the future trends for enterprise computing. Many of these are at the early adopter stage or are still in the realm of academic and scientific research and have yet to cross over into the mainstream business world. By studying some of these emerging and future trends, we can see how enterprise computing may evolve in the coming years. The technologies span the entire value chain of computing from core computing and networks, to devices and sensors, to new forms of user interfaces and human–computer interaction.

On the core computing and networks side, initiatives such as grid computing and power line networking are starting to challenge how we think about the way in which computing power and resources are accessed and how they are delivered. Grid computing enables us to tap into computing resources upon demand, much like traditional utilities such as water, gas, telephone, and electricity. Power line networking is starting to blur the lines between electrical power delivery and information delivery. With network access available over standard electrical cabling in the home, consumers will be able to connect a myriad of devices and appliances into a readily available network with minimal setup required, if and when this technology takes off.

On the device side, there are changes underway that will allow multimedia interaction on cell phones, new devices for managing personal area networks via gateways that serve as single connection points to the wireless carrier networks, and new forms of battery power such as fuel cells that can last three to five times the length of traditional lithium-ion batteries. Sensors can help us to detect microlevel changes to environmental attributes such as temperature and pressure, or even chemical changes. This helps to connect the physical world and its characteristics to the digital world for an increased understanding of our environmental or business context.

On the user interfaces and human–computer interaction side, there are many exciting developments under way. Artificial intelligence is applied for a variety of business productivity applications, including improved search capabilities, email filtering and prioritization, system troubleshooting, meeting facilitation, data mining, multimodal interfaces, and notification platforms. Multimodal interfaces can combine multiple interaction modes such as computer vision and speech recognition together with intelligent data analysis in order to help computers understand more about a business user's context and priorities. By observing user behavior, a computer can make determinations such as whether the person is in a meeting or is focused on solo activity at his or her personal computer. Speech recognition is used to improve the usability of handheld wireless devices with server-side voice recognition, streamed wirelessly from the device, being used to offload the processing requirements on the device itself. These types of behind-the-scenes intelligence engines are then applied in order to maximize the user's productivity in terms of automating tasks, prioritizing notifications and minimizing interruptions.

In effect, the computing industry is starting to give back some of the productivity that it took away from us in making us orient our work activities around computers in the first place. Computers have produced considerable automation in the business world, but they have also required us to orient our activities around them, especially over the past decade. Some of these future trends help to free us from these restraints by providing business information in more efficient and effective ways.

# Core Computing and Networks

## Grid Computing and Computing On Demand

Grid computing involves the application of distributed computing resources for the more efficient usage of processing, storage, applications, and data and for computing on demand. It represents a trend toward the use of information technology as a utility, with resources available upon demand and businesses paying for what they consume. Grid computing has the potential to reshape the entire application service provider and application infrastructure provider market. It changes our typical assumptions about how services are delivered and which services can be made available. Grid computing is similar to peer-to-peer technologies in that it can apply distributed computing resources working together to perform complex calculations and benefit from economies of scale. The difference is that while peer-to-peer technologies typically involve desktop computers running at the so-called "edge" of the network, the grid computing concept is more typically a collection of servers. As such, it can provide greater levels of security and manageability and is closer to the traditional outsourcing model.

Grid computing started in the academic and scientific domains via initiatives such as the Global Grid Forum, but it is now becoming available and of interest and benefit to the mainstream business as well. Companies such as Compaq, IBM, Microsoft, and Sun all have initiatives aimed at the enterprise offering a return on information technology investment in the form of computing utility services and software. The advantage to the business user is that of being able to tap into additional computing resources upon demand, based upon fluctuations in usage. The business can also minimize additional investments in computing resources when step-changes occur. When a usage and capacity threshold is reached, the business can tap into the "grid" instead of purchasing additional hardware. Businesses can also make better use of their own internal computing resources by setting up their own grids in order to tap unused processing cycles and storage. One of the barriers to adoption of grid computing is that it involves the sharing of computing resources, which brings up a number of security, manageability, and trust issues. Businesses may be willing to apply the technology within their own global network infrastructure or from the network of a trusted service provider, but obviously not from an untrusted, undefined network of servers scattered across the Internet. They will also be unlikely to want to share their own computing resources with others unless they are trusted business partners or customers. Some of the advantages and disadvantages of grid computing and computing on demand will be discussed later in this section, but first it's worth reviewing the current landscape in terms of academic and scientific initiatives and the industrial offerings available.

Academic and scientific initiatives in the grid computing arena include the Global Grid Forum and the Globus Project. The Global Grid Forum (GGF) is a community of working groups that are developing standards and best practices for distributed computing. The GGF was formed in November 2000 by merging the efforts of the North American "Grid Forum," the European Grid Forum "eGRID," and the Asia-Pacific grid community. Members of the GGF include over 200 organizations from over 30 countries.

The Globus Project is a research and development project that was started in 1996 and is centered at Argonne National Laboratory, the University of Southern California, and the University of Chicago. Research is supported by DARPA, the U.S. Department of Energy, NASA, the National Science Foundation, IBM, and Microsoft. The project is focused on enabling the application of grid computing concepts to scientific and engineering computing. The Globus Toolkit is software that enables organizations to set up their own grid computing infrastructure and to allow others to access their resources. Sites within the grid environment are able to maintain control over who has access to their computing resources via site administration tools. The toolkit includes components to help manage resource allocation, set up security infrastructure, access secondary storage, and to monitor the heartbeat of application processes. The toolkit has been widely adopted by a number of technology providers such as Compaq, IBM, Microsoft, and Sun as an open standard for grid computing. The toolkit is now evolving toward a standard called the Open Grid Services Architecture (OGSA), which combines grid computing concepts with Web services concepts for interoperability.

On the industry side, Compaq's Computing On Demand strategy offers enterprise customers increased flexibility and control over the design, management, and cost of their information technology infrastructure. The program was introduced in July 2001 and allows users to scale computing power based upon their needs. The program offers both capacity on demand and access on demand. The capacity on demand offering includes pay-per-use storage management and capacity, and pay-per-use measured processor (CPU) consumption. The access on demand offering includes per seat/per month thin client access, PC access, and mobile computing access. It allows businesses to scale the amount of user access they have to centralized server-based applications such as call center applications. Current customers of the Compaq Computing On Demand program include American Express, Bank of America, Franklin Templeton Investments, and Ericsson.

IBM's offering is called e-business on demand. The aim is to make e-business as convenient as accessing traditional utilities such as water, gas, telephone, and electricity. The e-business on demand offering is divided into infrastructure on demand and business process on demand. Infrastructure on demand includes core infrastructure services such as content distribution, Internet data and document exchange, managed hosting and storage, together with management services. Business process on demand includes horizontal business services such as business intelligence, e-commerce and e-procurement, together with industry-specific services such as communications, distribution, industrial, and finance. As part of this initiative, IBM has invested over $4 billion to build more data centers worldwide.

Sun's offering in the grid computing space is comprised of a combination of hardware and software products. The main software product is Grid Engine software that provides a distributed resource management application for grid computing. It includes specialized software agents on each machine that can help to identify and deliver the available computing resources for the grid environment. Customers using the grid engine software include companies in electronic design automation, mechanical computer-aided engineering, biotechnology, and scientific research. Sun has also released the grid engine software source code into the broad open-source community via their grid engine project. In addition to the grid engine software, Sun also has a variety of software products for managing grid infrastructure, grid security, and grid systems management. Practicing the technology itself, Sun uses a 4,000 processor campus grid, with a 98 percent CPU utilization, to execute over 50,000 electronic design automation jobs a day. For most businesses, typical CPU utilizations for workstations and servers range from five to twenty percent, so this type of usage level helps to maximize existing investments in servers and helps to avoid investments in supercomputers.

One of the business scenarios to which grid computing can be applied is within a shared services IT environment. Many large corporations provide shared IT services to their operating companies. These operating companies can often number into the tens or even hundreds within a single corporation. A shared IT services environment helps to reduce costs by leveraging prepurchased enterprise software licenses, computing infrastructure, and staffing. In addition, best practices and templates for software development, deployment, and ongoing operations can be developed and shared across all operating companies. These shared services models can establish application service provider and application infrastructure provider services and offer grid computing as an additional value-added service. Computing resources such as processing time and disk space may not be completely utilized in the shared services environment via traditional hosted applications. Grid computing provides a way for the additional capacity to be tapped into and consumed upon demand, thus maximizing the use of existing IT assets and infrastructure such as servers and storage.

One of the challenges for such a shared services environment offering computing resources is to develop the usage and pricing model that will recover costs and charge the various operating companies appropriate amounts based upon their level of consumption.

In fact, this is a challenge that faces the entire computing utility movement, not just IT shared services environments. As one starts to offer per-transaction and per-usage pricing models, there is an increasing need to better track and report on such usage. Most software licensing products were developed to support the concept of one-time shrink-wrapped software product sales rather than the emerging software as a service model. In addition, usage levels will vary by customer or by operating company, so it becomes important for usage to be accurately measured and reported for fair pricing among customers.

The appropriate measurement attributes that are cost drivers will also vary by application category. For example, packaged applications typically have the number of end users as a primary cost driver. This is generally easy to report on since the number of end users can be tracked by the number of software licenses granted or the number of registered users in a database. Customers also like to see consistent and predictable pricing, and per-user pricing provides this and eliminates surprises due to variations in usage. The cost drivers for lower level infrastructure applications are typically harder-to-measure attributes such as number of servers, number of processors, and number of transactions. They may be independent of the actual number of end users and may consume a variety of resources such as processing power, disk space, and bandwidth. Once this is measured, there is still the challenge of providing customers with monthly bills that may vary greatly. While these types of bills can be considered "fair," they are often undesirable due to the difficulty of predicting charges for budgeting purposes.

Another challenge for service providers is the ability to put in place sophisticated provisioning and billing applications that can automate the provision of service, track usage, and charge for the services via a complex set of usage measurement attributes. As software becomes more like a traditional utility, software services providers will need to build the same types of operational support systems (OSS) and business support systems (BSS) that the wireless carriers currently use when delivering wireless service to their subscribers. Wireless carriers have streamlined and automated their services in order to bring on new customers with minimal cost. Software services providers offering grid computing capabilities and IT utility capabilities will need to develop similar turn-key approaches to adopting customers into their environments in order to make their ventures profitable.

The general business trend that is occurring with grid computing appears to be the increasing distribution of processing for economies of scale and the increasing granularity of services offered. Instead of tapping into application services only, businesses can now tap into IT utility services such as additional processing power, disk space, and bandwidth. The fundamental challenges for this model include trust and security as the computing grid expands and migrates toward a global network, often crossing various organizational boundaries. Businesses can benefit from on-demand service if their grid computing or IT utility is outsourced, but they will have the same management, security, and trust issues as with any other type of external provider. To be successful, service providers must provide management tools for their customers for self-administration of certain common tasks, strong service level agreements for availability and notification and response time for planned and unplanned outages, and high levels of security within their infrastructure. This is true whether the service is a third-party offering or an internal IT shared services offering.

## Power Line Networking

With ever more devices and appliances such as consumer electronics becoming data enabled, one of the challenges for manufacturers, retailers, service providers, and consumers is how to provide these devices with connectivity within the home. In fact, according to the analyst group Cahners In-Stat, the home connectivity market is expected to reach $6 billion by 2004. Connectivity can enable device-to-device communications, for example, for use in gaming applications, in addition to communications with the Internet for remote monitoring purposes and data exchange. In the consumer home networking arena, many techniques currently exist for users to network their computers and appliances. In addition to traditional wired, or Ethernet, connections that operate at ten megabits per second, consumers now have options such as wireless networking via a variety of wireless standards such as 802.11b (also sometimes known as Wi-Fi, which is the certification standard for 802.11b compatibility) or Bluetooth and options such as connecting via standard telephone lines. The HomePNA standard allows devices to be networked across home telephone sockets. HomePNA is the Home Phoneline Networking Alliance, which is a nonprofit association of industry companies such as 3Com, Agere Systems, AMD, AT&T Wireless Services, Broadcom, Compaq, Conexant, Hewlett-Packard, Intel, Motorola, and 2Wire. The association was founded in June 1998, has over 150 member companies, and has released two specifications for home networking at one megabit per second and ten megabits per second via the standard RJ-11 phone jack. Their third-generation specification will target multimedia applications at 100 megabits per second. Products available for this network include preconfigured PCs, network interface cards, routers, modems, and Internet appliances.

A new alternative to Ethernet, wireless, and phone line networks, called power line networking, promises to offer a new way to connect appliances in the home using existing copper-wire infrastructure. It actually uses the electrical wiring system already installed in the home in order to provide the network connection via any electrical outlet. One of the benefits of this method is the ubiquity of connections already installed in the home, often two or more electrical outlets per room compared to just a handful of phone line connections per entire home. This option is also a more secure approach than wireless networking via 802.11b or Bluetooth, which spreads the data signal in an uncontrolled dispersion pattern to anyone within the signal radius wanting to listen in on the communications. For 802.11b, this signal can travel up to 500 feet indoors or 1,000 feet outdoors. Bluetooth is a shorter range wireless networking specification that can travel about 33 feet or 10 meters. It should be noted that many vendors such as Credant Technologies are attacking the wireless security market with products that help to ensure the confidentiality of data via access control and encryption.

One of the challenges of delivering data over the power supply is that these types of networks are very noisy and variable in terms of interference since they were not designed to carry digital data transmissions. When electrical devices are turned on and off, they can cause spikes and other noise patterns that can distort the electrical signal and the data signal that is riding along with it.

The HomePlug Powerline Alliance is a consortium of companies that is aiming to develop new standards for power line networking and has overcome many of these original technical difficulties. The Alliance is a nonprofit industry association comprised of over 90 companies that was formed in April 2000. Some of the original founding companies included 3Com, AMD, Cisco Systems, Conexant, Enikia, Intel, Intellon, Motorola, Panasonic, S3's Diamond Multimedia, RadioShack, and Texas Instruments. Many of these companies are also playing a role in the Home Phoneline Networking Alliance and are obviously hedging their bets as to which will generate the most traction in the consumer marketplace. Most of them will benefit from the adoption of either technology since they stand to sell more network interface cards and other forms of networking equipment. The HomePlug 1.0 specification provides a data rate of 14 megabits per second and supports products for gaming, consumer electronics, voice telephony, and personal computing. The group has already conducted field trials within the United States and has confirmed that the specification is ready for market rollout. The next steps will be the introduction of HomePlug-compliant products from its member companies and continued work to ensure product compatibility.

For businesses in the consumer electronics arena, the advent of power line networking and other forms of networking within the home open up new possibilities for providing service to consumers. If consumers have a cable modem or DSL router, they can connect a power line router and instantly have full Internet access across the home. Intelligent devices and appliances are then able to be accessed from remote locations. Consumers can manage home security settings and lighting settings. Retailers can offer value-added data services for their smart appliances and can troubleshoot appliances remotely and potentially eliminate on-site visits. Some potential future scenarios include refrigerators that can reorder supplies, music systems that can purchase and play music downloaded from the Internet from legal music sites, gaming systems that can purchase and install new games, and a variety of home systems such as air conditioning, electrical, and security settings that can be remotely administered. Of course, one of the challenges is that with more devices exposed on the Internet, the potential for unauthorized usage can have far more severe effects than the relatively benign email issues from viruses that we see today. One can imagine alarms being deactivated, air-conditioning systems turned off, or ovens being set on high. Any home networking solution that enables home appliances to be remotely managed via the Internet needs to have stringent controls in terms of user authentication and access control. As the home, in addition to the office, becomes increasingly connected, the need for robust security will be a key requirement in order to spur user adoption. Without adequate security, these innovations may be relegated to niche markets and may miss out on widespread consumer acceptance.

# Devices and Sensors

## Devices

Devices are changing forms and functionality as manufacturers attempt to increase their usability and functionality for various enterprise and consumer scenarios. Smartphones, the combined cellular phone and PDA devices, are just one example. Devices such as Nokia's 9290 Communicator are fully integrated mobile terminals running the Symbian operating system that combines phone, fax, email, calendar, and imaging functionality into a single device. Kyocera's QCP 6035 smartphone combines a CDMA digital wireless phone with a Palm OS handheld computer. Ericsson's R380 is another example of a smartphone having PDA functionality and running on GSM networks. For the business user, the smartphone may well enable the enterprise to standardize on fewer devices for their corporate users. Fewer devices translates into reduced purchase and support costs and increased productivity for employees.

Beyond the cell phone and PDA combination, companies such as Samsung have introduced concept phones, including watch phones, camera phones, and TV phones. Multimedia messaging using the Multimedia Messaging Service (MMS) standard is being used to transform cell phones into communications devices that can exchange audio, images, and other forms of rich content. Companies such as Nokia already have MMS-enabled phones such as the 7650 with a built-in digital camera that are in use on live networks in Europe.

Wearable devices are a future trend as mobile devices morph into the ultimate in mobility by becoming wearable as gloves, headsets, and so forth. Wearable devices benefit the end user by being located at the point of activity without interfering with the activity at hand. They can provide improved interactivity and flexibility over the traditional mobile devices or the traditional keyboard and monitor. Essentially, they provide the advantages of automation without the disadvantage of the process change to accommodate the technology.

Manufacturers are also experimenting with how all these devices such as phones, watches, and cameras may eventually connect into the wireless network. As the number of devices per user proliferates, each device with its own built-in wireless networking capabilities becomes a redundant and costly proposition for end users. A potential new solution is to have a networking device that is separate from the end devices themselves. In this way, devices can become smaller, more functional, more fashionable in the case of consumer-oriented brands, and less costly. The networking device performs the required wireless connectivity on their behalf. The end devices simply communicate with this networking device via short-range wireless protocols such as Bluetooth. An example of a software company providing this type of solution is IXI Mobile. The company offers a personal mobile gateway (PMG) that acts as a bridge between the devices and the wireless network. The PMG can be a standalone device or can be incorporated into a battery pack or existing cellular phones. The interesting theme here is that this concept separates the communications requirements from the form and functional requirements of the devices themselves. It therefore allows devices to be manufactured with lower costs and a faster time to market and serves as the gateway between the short-range personal area network and the wide area network provided by the wireless carriers.

One of the challenges with portable devices has always been battery life. As portable devices such as handheld personal computers, cell phones, and personal digital assistants gain ever more functionality, they also become an increasing drain on battery power. Fuel cells are an emerging technology that provides much longer life than traditional lithium-ion batteries. They can last three to five times longer and are more environmentally friendly. Fuel cells are electrochemical devices that run on hydrogen, methanol, propane, butane, or other similar sources by converting chemical energy into electrical energy with by-products of water and carbon dioxide. One of the companies manufacturing fuel cells is Smart Fuel Cell GmbH, based in Munich. The company targets devices such as notebooks, camcorders and power tools and began pilot production and field trials with industry partners in early 2002.

## Sensors

RFID chips were discussed in the chapter on mobile business. Beyond RFID chips are a wide array of other intelligent sensors. These sensors are capable of detecting changes in the physical environment such as temperature and pressure, and even detecting chemical particles. When sensors are deployed in a net of 10s, 100s, or 1,000s, they can provide us with valuable information about our environment, and activities and changes occurring within that environment over time. These types of sensors and their corresponding detection events can be applied for environmental monitoring and protection, transportation, medicine, and even homeland security. They can help to detect microlevel changes that often escape the human eye, but which can signal broader macroscale impacts. In essence, these sensors help us to connect the physical environment to the virtual computing network of people and applications. By adding the physical element, we are creating a more accurate picture of our business world within the digital world and are able to make more informed decisions from a greater range of input parameters. The addition of sensors providing input parameters to business systems can help us to extend our virtual radar in the e-business world and to react more swiftly to threats and opportunities that would have previously passed unnoticed. Sensors can provide continual information on business events that help to add a historical perspective on how objects and environmental factors have varied in terms of location and core attributes over time. This contributes substantially to an improved understanding of "context" for both business applications and scientific applications.

# User Interfaces and Human–Computer Interaction

In addition to developments in core computing and networking technologies such as grid computing and power line networking, and advances in devices and sensors, changes are underway for the way in which we interact with computers. For a long time, we have relied upon the keyboard, mouse, graphical user interface, and the general desktop metaphor. The new advances in human–computer interaction will enable faster and more effective forms of interaction that incorporate speech recognition, natural language processing, artificial intelligence, and new forms of visual interfaces that go beyond the traditional desktop metaphor.

## Artificial Intelligence

The work on artificial intelligence has historically focused on attempting to make computers think like humans, giving them the ability to learn, reason, and to create. One of the best-known examples from science fiction was the movie *2001* that portrayed HAL, a computer with artificial intelligence that was able to see and hear, talk, reason, plan, and even lip-read. While the industry has not been successful in creating a computer with such all-round capabilities as in the vision laid out by HAL, there have been many successes in focused areas where computers have been able to apply their massive processing capability. For example, IBM's Deep Blue computer system was designed to play chess at the Grand Master level and indeed defeated the reigning World Chess Champion, Garry Kasparov, in May 1997. The Deep Blue computer, a massively parallel RS/6000 SP computer system, was able to examine and evaluate up to 200 million chess positions per second. On the IBM research Web site, the company has pointed out that while Deep Blue is highly effective at solving chess problems, it is not a "learning system" and has limited intelligence when compared to human beings.

Even though computers have not been able to think in the same manner as the human brain and to apply common sense and language understanding, they can be applied using their own strengths and characteristics in order to solve a variety of everyday tasks. In this way, artificial intelligence is increasingly being applied in a number of business scenarios in order to improve productivity and decision-making ability. A well-known example is the Microsoft Office Assistant, the animated character that offers help when performing various tasks within programs such as Microsoft Word. It can aid in troubleshooting by asking a series of questions related to the task at hand. Microsoft Windows XP uses additional artificial intelligence capabilities such as a tool called Search Companion that can aid with searches on the computer, home or office network, or the Internet. More recent examples can be found in some of the projects that Microsoft Research is conducting. The group is applying artificial intelligence to a variety of productivity applications including improved search capabilities, email filtering and prioritization, system troubleshooting, meeting facilitation, data mining, multimodal interfaces, and notification platforms.

Artificial intelligence can be applied to improve worker productivity when using email and other applications by helping to prioritize the most important messages and tasks. Software can look at various aspects of an email message such as the subject line and text within the email, the relationship between the sender and the worker in terms of the company organization chart, and the history of communications between these individuals, including the response times, in order to determine how important a communication may be and the potential costs of a delayed response. Microsoft's Priorities system does just this. The goal is to help users get the right information at the right time on the right device. The Priorities system is part of a larger project named the Notification Platform. This platform, being developed by Microsoft Research, is part of their Attentional User Interface (AUI) project, which focuses on attention- and context-sensitive costs and benefits of information and services. The Priorities system goes well beyond analysis of an email message when determining a priority and deciding when to alert an end user to the arrival of an incoming message. It actually uses a number of HAL-like techniques to determine the user's context and readiness to be alerted to an inbound priority message. Beyond email, the inbound message could be a telephone call, an instant message, or an information feed. The system visually observes the user's activity, listens to the surrounding sounds, checks the user's calendar and makes decisions as to the appropriate timing and manner in which to deliver information. In observing the user's activity, the system uses a Bayesian vision system to determine the context of activity. Thomas Bayes was an English mathematician in the 18th century who established a mathematical basis for probability inference. Bayesian systems are based upon his theories of statistical probability. The context of the user's activity can be determined by observing where the user's attention is focused. If the user is looking constantly at the computer screen, then it is likely he or she is working on some solo activity on the computer. If the user is away from the screen and the system observes several faces in the room, then it is likely the user is in some form of meeting and does not want to be disturbed. By adding information from the user's calendar and audio information to this analysis, the system is able to make even more informed decisions. Should these systems become commercialized in the future, the challenge will be to ensure user confidence in the privacy of information observed. Employees may well fear that this type of information could be used to report back to management on their behavior and general productivity.

## Speech Technology

Speech technology incorporates a number of disciplines aimed at spoken language technologies. It can include speech recognition, speech synthesis (text-to-speech), speaker identification, and multimodal technologies that combine speech with other forms of user interaction in order to enhance the computing environment for end users. Multimodal technologies are particularly interesting because they can help make devices more usable. For example, personal digital assistants are useful for highly mobile employees due to their portability and wireless connectivity, but are often difficult to use in terms of data entry. Inputting large amounts of text is difficult using handwriting recognition or the graphical software-based keyboard. In this situation, speech recognition can be applied in order to improve the input capabilities of these devices and make them much easier to use. Combined with natural language processing, end users can essentially talk to their devices and have the device understand the intended meaning of their commands. Since mobile devices are often underpowered to perform continuous speech recognition by themselves, techniques such as distributed speech recognition can be applied to stream the audio signal back to a server computer for processing and interpretation over the wireless network and then to execute the required command back on the mobile device. This type of technique can be applied for general dictation as well as more advanced functionality such as meeting scheduling. Tasks such as scheduling can be made more accurate by combining modalities. For example, a user can verbally request a meeting but tap certain areas of his or her calendar at the same time in order to provide more guidance to the computer.

Text-to-speech capabilities enable a number of useful scenarios as well. For example, individuals driving in their car or using their cell phone can listen to email as it is read by a text-to-speech converter. Based on the current device in use and the user's activity or context, various forms of interaction can be the most optimal mode of human–computer interaction.

An interesting extension of speech technology and multimodal technologies is that they can be decoupled from the actual device in use and become part of a computer-based service running on the network that can follow the users around as they move from their homes to their cars and to their offices. It becomes a virtual assistant that follows the user's context and can aid with a variety of tasks regardless of the current device being used.

Microsoft Research has a project called Dr. Who that is investigating these types of opportunities. They see the service becoming a Web service that is specialized in a particular domain such as scheduling and can be looped into human conversations in order to execute a task. For example, the service could be asked to find a certain type of restaurant within close proximity. One can also imagine location-based services being applied to automatically determine the user's current location. It's easy to see that, when location-based services, Web services, and multimodal user interaction techniques are combined, they start to open up powerful opportunities for computers to create new forms of value that can improve productivity.

## Visual Interfaces

A final area within the category of user interfaces and human–computer interaction is the actual visual interface itself. The screen is the primary way in which we communicate with the computer in terms of our day-to-day activities. These typically involve actions such as reading, writing, managing and organizing content, interacting with others, and receiving notifications related to emails, instant messaging, alerts, and appointments. One of the issues over the past several years has been the ever-increasing stream of information flow in the form of notifications that have the potential to distract us from our primary work activities. A constant flood of email alerts and other forms of notification throughout the day can be a large distraction for most knowledge workers.

Several major companies such as IBM and Microsoft, together with numerous startups, are currently looking into new ways to present information and maximize the quality of information conveyed while minimizing effort on the part of the end user. If smarter visual interfaces can be developed that can present more information more rapidly or in a more accessible manner, then they can have a significant effect on productivity.

One example is the Scope application from Microsoft Research. The scope is designed to summarize a variety of notifications into a glanceable visualization tool. Figure 9-1 shows a sample of the interface. Notifications are grouped into alerts, inbox items such as emails, calendar items, and tasks. Objects near the center of the scope are the higher priority items. The notifications can be prioritized using the Microsoft notification platform and priorities system that was discussed earlier. These systems apply artificial intelligence techniques in order to determine the relative priority of one task over another. Users can select and zoom in on notifications using the Scope and drill down into them in order to gain more details. As we adapt our work habits around computing, research projects such as Scope have the potential to help gain back some of the time and attention that is spent in switching between various activities and in making decisions as to task priorities.

For many years, we have relied upon the desktop metaphor of Microsoft Windows and the Macintosh. These are two-dimensional metaphors for managing documents and applications. Microsoft Research is also looking into ways we can apply three-dimensional graphics in order to increase productivity around information management and to make the desktop metaphor more intuitive. Their TaskGallery research prototype uses a three-dimensional office metaphor instead of a two-dimensional desktop. Objects can be placed on the walls, ceiling, or floor of this 3D space and can be ordered by depth. The TaskGallery also provides an interesting transition vehicle for 2D to 3D migration in terms of user adoption due to the ability to bring unmodified Windows applications into the environment.

**Figure 9-1**  The "Scope" Glanceable Notification Summarizer from Microsoft Research. Source: Microsoft.

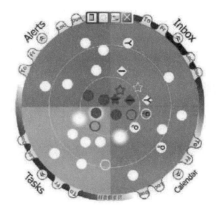

Other technologies in the visual interface category include the Scopeware product from Mirror Worlds Technologies and the Star Tree product from Inxight. Scopeware is a knowledge management solution that locates and presents business information in more accessible formats for end users. One of the Scopeware products is Scopeware Mobile. The solution provides mobile users with a "rolling window around now"—a stream of their most relevant information that is updated on a real-time basis. The core platform offered by Scopeware is their Information Management Infrastructure, or IMI. This platform aims to increase the value of information by making it more searchable and accessible. Inxight's products aid in unstructured data management by providing software for analyzing, organizing, categorizing, and navigating information. Their Star Tree product helps companies navigate and visualize large hierarchies of information. Figure 9-2 shows a sample Web site published as a Star Tree. Studies at Xerox PARC have shown the Star Tree technology to be 62 percent more effective than Windows tree controls when navigating collections of Web pages.

While visual interfaces are often overlooked due to the dominance of operating system platforms such as Microsoft Windows and the

**Figure 9-2**  The "Star Tree" Viewer Technology from Inxight. Source: Inxight.

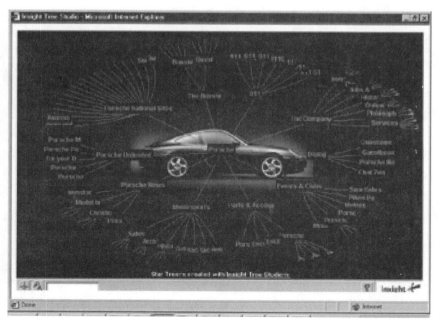

Macintosh, it is important for businesses to stay tuned to some of these emerging developments and alternative solutions. While they may not replace well-established modes of visual interaction with Web pages and with the traditional desktop, they can very well be applied in order to enhance the experience. In certain specialty applications, they can also be the most optimal solution for navigating and visualizing large amounts of data—helping to turn the data into meaningful information that can enable business understanding and business decisions.

This snapshot of some of the future trends in computing has aimed to illustrate where some of the developments are actually occurring. There are obviously many other areas that are equally or even more important. The general theme is that the trends cover the network layer, the hardware layer, and the software layer. Gradually, the computing options available to business users are becoming more flexible, more open, more intelligent, and more usable. The way in which we interact with computers and the way in which our customers and business partners interact with computers are changing. We are finally gaining the ability to deliver the right information to the right person at the right time. This is a capability that will be a key competitive advantage for businesses in the future.

# Extending the Radar Lessons

>>   Future trends in computing span the entire value chain from core computing and networks, to devices and sensors, to new forms of user interfaces and human–computer interaction.

>>   Grid computing enables us to tap into computing resources upon demand much like traditional utilities such as water, gas, telephone, and electricity.

>>   Power line networking is starting to blur the lines between electrical power delivery and data delivery.

>>   Wearable devices are a future trend as mobile devices morph into the ultimate in mobility by becoming wearable as gloves, headsets, and other form factors. Wearable devices provide the advantages of automation without the disadvantage of the process change to accommodate the technology.

>> Fuel cells are an emerging technology that provides much longer life than traditional lithium-ion batteries They can last three to five times longer and are more environmentally friendly.

>> Artificial intelligence is being applied for a variety of business productivity applications including improved search capabilities, email filtering and prioritization, system troubleshooting, meeting facilitation, data mining, multimodal interfaces, and notification platforms.

>> Multimodal interfaces can combine multiple interaction modes such as computer vision and speech recognition together with intelligent data analysis in order to help computers understand more about a business user's context and priorities.

>> Speech recognition is being used improve the usability of handheld wireless devices with server-side voice recognition, streamed wirelessly from the device, being used to offload the processing requirements on the device itself.

# Extending the Radar Considerations

>> How can grid computing and computing on demand be applied to your business? Which processes require intensive computing power or vary greatly in their utilization of computing resources?

>> How can wearable devices be applied within your business operations in order to streamline processes and to reduce costs?

>> How can artificial intelligence be applied for productivity improvements within your business?

>> How can multimodal interfaces improve productivity for knowledge workers and highly mobile employees within your business?

# Chapter

# 10

# Conclusion

*"This is not the end, it is not even the beginning of the end.
But it is, perhaps, the end of the beginning."*

—Sir Winston Churchill

H aving arrived at the end of our journey through the world of emerging and disruptive technologies, it's worth examining where we stand in the current evolution of information technology and how the next several years may impact our businesses. The outstanding question is whether or not the next five years will be as dramatic as the past five years in terms of the highs and lows of our expectations, business objectives and realities, and economic forecasts. We also need to know whether the next five years will bring increased business productivity from the application of technology or whether the gains have already been accomplished. Is the Internet technology wave just starting or has it already peaked? What were the lessons learned over the past several years and how can these be applied moving forward? Where can new forms of value be extracted and how should an organization position itself to gain competitive advantage? What is the future role and impact of technology for achieving competitive advantage? What is the next killer application and what is the timing of consumer and enterprise adoption?

I hope this book has demonstrated that we are just beginning to extract true business benefit from Internet-based technologies and applications. The technology is still relatively new on the scene and the past five or more years have been, for the most part, a learning period. We've learned what works and what doesn't work and have seen just a few companies and solutions really make it through the first hurdle. In the dot-com space, we've seen companies such as Amazon.com and eBay succeed. In the enterprise space, we've seen software packages such as enterprise resource planning, customer relationship management, and supply chain management transform our businesses even if they haven't yet met expectations for returns. According to Ray Lane, a venture capitalist with Kleiner Perkins, Caufield & Byers, and former President and Chief Operating Officer of Oracle Corporation, the next five years will give us a chance to go in and test these applications to see how well they are providing real business performance and functionality at lower cost. We've changed the way in which we deliver value to customers, suppliers, and business partners; now it is time to refine and optimize our model.

The next wave of technologies that I have outlined in this book represents what we might call round two of the Internet era. Technology companies have gone back in and refined how applications and business processes should really work when delivered over the Internet. The first wave of applications was essentially a forced fit on top of a powerful but vulnerable framework. This next wave of innovation will help to increase our confidence in conducting business electronically and also to create new ways for us to extract new forms of business value. It may be hard to predict the exact timing for adoption of some of these technologies such as mobile commerce or radio frequency identification, but they all serve as strategic enablers for us to create value and improve productivity. We are entering an era of combinations, an era where killer applications are built from combinations of killer technologies, where computers can start to serve their users rather than command their users, where information and transactions are able to move seamlessly across location boundaries, device boundaries, and physical and virtual boundaries. Users will be able to interact with applications from any place, on any device, via any interface—whether it is a graphical interface or a spoken interface. Physical goods and assets will start to become part of the overall electronic fabric via electronic tagging and electronic product codes.

There will be an exponential increase in the number of electronic transactions. These transactions will migrate from the human-to-machine interactions of today to a mass of interrelationships and interactions among people, devices, appliances, computers, and intelligent objects.

These long-term trends are taking place today. Developments in the emerging and disruptive technologies that we have profiled, together with many other technologies that were not included, will pave the way toward mass adoption. Each technology is gaining a certain degree of lift in terms of adoption from other synergistic technologies. Web services will help to lift mobile business, radio frequency identification will help to lift real-time computing, and grid computing will help to lift computing utilities. By extending the radar and detecting these patterns early, the enterprise can be in the best position to sense and respond. It has been said that the best way to predict the future is to invent it. Millions of people and thousands of companies are inventing the future every day. By extending the radar function within your business, you will be able to detect some of the most important innovations that are occurring in the outside world ahead of time and will be able to create a powerful window of opportunity to prepare and act faster than your competition.

Since we are entering the truly productive phase of the Internet technology evolution, it is important to reshape the historical technology adoption curve within your business. If you are a mainstream enterprise, you need to become more like an early adopter. If you are an early adopter, you need to become more like a pioneer. Think of it not as a first-mover advantage but a smart-mover advantage.

Today, more than ever, it is important to realize that emerging and disruptive technologies can yield as much if not far more business value than today's mainstream applications. They can also be implemented in conjunction with your existing enterprise information technology infrastructure. Emerging technologies can provide you with an edge on your competition. Disruptive technologies can fundamentally change the rules of the game both for your business and for your entire industry. Even in a back-to-basics economic climate, these technologies hold the secret both to revenue generation and to cost reduction and performance improvement. How prepared is your radar?

# References

## Introduction

>> *"We ought not be over-anxious to encourage innovation, in case of doubtful improvement, for an old system must ever have two advantages over a new one; it is established and it is understood."*—C.C. Colton
The Quotations Page, *http://www.quotationspage.com*

## Chapter 1

>> *"Computing is rapidly approaching an inflection point where science fiction writers' predictions of helpful, ubiquitous and seamless technology will become a reality"*—Richard Rashid, Senior Vice President, Microsoft Research
"Bill Gates and Microsoft Research Chart the Future of Computing," Redmond Washington, September 5, 2001,
*http://www.microsoft.com/presspass/press/2001/sep01/09-05MSR10AnnivPR.asp*

>> Aberdeen Group, *http://www.aberdeen.com*
>> AMR Research, *http://www.amrresearch.com*
>> IDC, *http://www.idc.com*
>> Internet Week, *http://www.internetwk.com*
>> Internet2® Consortium, *http://www.internet2.org*
>> Meta Group, *http://www.metagroup.com*
>> mFormation Technologies, *http://www.mformation.com*
>> Red Herring, "Generation Now," July 15, 2001,
   *http://www.redherring.com*
>> U.S. Bureau of Labor Statistics, *http://stats.bls.gov*
>> Wired, "How CloudNine Wound Up in Hell," February 1, 2002,
   *http://www.wired.com/news/business/0,1367,50171,00.html*

# Chapter 2

>> *"As a result of the changes in how businesses and consumers use the
   Web, the industry is converging on a new computing model that enables
   a standard way of building applications and processes to connect and
   exchange information over the Web."*—Bill Gates, Microsoft
   "Bill Gates on Microsoft .NET Today," January 14, 2002,
   *http://www.microsoft.com/net/defined/net_today.asp*
>> Bowstreet, *http://www.bowstreet.com*
>> DuPont Performance Coatings,
   *http://www.performancecoatings.dupont.com*
>> Grand Central Communications, *http://www.grandcentral.com*
>> Hewlett-Packard, *http://www.hp.com*
>> IBM, *http://www.ibm.com*
>> mFormation Technologies, *http://www.mformation.com*
>> Microsoft, *http://www.microsoft.com*
>> Oracle, *http://www.oracle.com*
>> Sun, *http://www.sun.com*
>> UDDI, *http://www.uddi.org*
>> WS-I, *http://www.ws-i.org*

# Chapter 3

>> "Peer-to-peer computing is the revolution that could change computing
   as we know it."—Patrick Gelsinger, Chief Technology Officer, Intel
   "Software Technologies: Peer-to-Peer Computing Trends," Fall 2000,
   *http://cedar.intel.com/cgi-bin/ids.dll/topic.jsp?catCode=BYN*

>> Aberdeen Group, *http://www.aberdeen.com*

>> AMR Research, *http://www.amrresearch.com*

>> Groove Networks, *http://www.groove.net*

>> Intel NetBatch Case Study, *http://cedar.intel.com/cgi-bin/ids.dll/content/content.jsp?cntKey=Generic%20Editorial::p2p_netbatch&cntType=IDS_EDITORIAL&catCode=BYP*

>> Intel Peer-to-Peer Initiative, *http://cedar.intel.com/cgi-bin/ids.dll/topic.jsp?catCode=BYM*

>> Intel Peer-to-Peer Working Group, *http://www.p2pwg.org*

>> NextPage, *http://www.nextpage.com*

>> NextPage, Baker & McKenzie Case Study, *http://www.nextpage.com/document.asp?section=Customer&path=Customer/customer%-20stories/bnm.xml*

>> Sun Project JXTA, *http://www.jxta.org*

>> SETI@Home, *http://setiathome.ssl.berkeley.edu*

>> United Devices Anthrax Research Program, *http://www.ud.com*

# Chapter 4

>> *"There is never enough time, unless you're serving it."*—Malcolm Forbes
The Quotations Page,
*http://www.quotationspage.com/quotes/Malcolm_Forbes/*

>> Dell, *http://www.dell.com*

>> Gartner, "The Challenges of Real-Time Business," November 29, 2001, *http://www.gartner.com*

>> GlobeRanger, *http://www.globeranger.com*

>> Intrinsyc, *http://www.intrinsyc.com*

>> KnowNow, *http://www.knownow.com*

>> Office Depot, *http://www.officedepot.com*

# Chapter 5

>> *"If you can't describe what you are doing as a process, you don't know what you're doing."*—W. Edwards Deming
The Quotations Page, *http://www.quotationspage.com*

>> Business Process Management Initiative (BPMI.org), *http://www.bpmi.org*

>> CIO Magazine, *http://www.cio.com*

>> Exigen, *http://www.exigen.com*

>> Intalio, *http://www.intalio.com*

>> Zaplet, *http://www.zaplet.com*

# Chapter 6

>> *"The only way to discover the limits of the possible is to go beyond them into the impossible."*—Arthur C. Clarke
   Arthur C. Clarke, "Technology and the Future," The Quotations Page, *http://www.quotationspage.com/quotes/Arthur_C_Clarke/*
>> Apple, *http://www.apple.com*
>> ARC Group, *http://www.arcgroup.com*
>> Cahners In-Stat Group, *http://www.instat.com*
>> Chrysler, *http://www.chrysler.com*
>> EE Times, "Euro bank notes to embed RFID chips by 2005," December 19, 2001, *http://www.eetimes.com/story/OEG20011219S0016*
>> FCC, *http://www.fcc.gov*
>> Ford, *http://www.ford.com*
>> Gartner, *http://www.gartner.com*
>> Honda, *http://www.honda.com*
>> Location Inter-operability Forum (LIF), *www.locationforum.org*
>> Mercedes Benz, *http://www.mercedes-benz.com*
>> mFormation Technologies, *http://www.mformation.com*
>> Microsoft Car.Net, *http://www.microsoft.com/presspass/press/2000/Oct00/CarNetPR.asp*
>> M.I.T. Auto-ID Center, *http://www.autoidcenter.com*
>> Nokia, *http://www.nokia.com*
>> Texas Instruments, TI*RFID, *http://www.ti.com/tiris*
>> U.S. Army & Bees, *http://www.pnl.gov/breakthroughs/fall99/critical.html*
>> Volvo, *http://www.volvo.com*
>> Wingcast, *www.wingcast.com*

# Chapter 7

>> *"You ask, what is our aim? I can answer in one word: Victory—victory at all costs, victory in spite of all terror, victory, however long and hard the road may be; without victory, there is no survival."*
   —Sir Winston Churchill
   "Winston Churchill Quotations," Jarrold Publishing, 1997
>> CERT, *http://www.cert.org*
>> Check Point Software Technologies, *http://www.checkpoint.com*
>> Computer Security Institute, *http://www.csi.org*

>> The Department of Homeland Security,
*http://www.whitehouse.gov/deptofhomeland/*
>> FBI, *http://www.fbi.gov*
>> IBM UltraPort, *http://www.pc.ibm.com/us/accessories/thinkpad.html*
>> Liberty Alliance, *http://www.projectliberty.org*
>> Microsoft Passport,
*http://www.passport.com/Consumer/default.asp?lc=1033*
>> Microsoft Secure Windows Initiative, *http://www.microsoft.com/Press-Pass/press/2001/Apr01/04-10ThompsonPR.asp*
>> Microsoft Trustworthy Computing, *http://www.microsoft.com/press-pass/exec/craig/05-01trustworthywp.asp*
>> National Security Agency, *http://www.nsa.gov*
>> RSA, *http://www.rsa.com*
>> Tripwire, *http://www.tripwire.com*
>> Viisage Technology, *http://www.viisage.com*
>> Visionics, *http://www.visionics.com*

# Chapter 8

>> *"Perception is strong and sight weak. In strategy it is important to see distant things as if they were close and to take a distanced view of close things."*—Miyamoto Musashi
Miyamoto Musashi (1584–1645), The Quotations Page,
*http://www.quotationspage.com*
>> Introduction to Naval Weapons Engineering, Federation of American Scientists, *http://www.fas.org/man/dod-101/navy/docs/es310/radarsys/radarsys.htm*
>> M.I.T. Technology Review, Corporate R&D Scorecard 2001,
*http://www.technologyreview.com*

# Chapter 9

>> *"I am a HAL Nine Thousand computer, Production Number 3. I became operational at the HAL Plant in Urbana, Illinois, on January 12, 1997."*—2001: A Space Odyssey
HAL, 2001: A Space Odyssey (the novel),
*http://mitpress.mit.edu/e-books/Hal/preface/preface1.html*
>> Bluetooth, *www.bluetooth.com*
>> Credant Technologies, *http://www.credant.com/*

>> Compaq Computing On Demand, *http://www.compaq.com/cod/*
>> Global Grid Forum, *www.globalgridforum.org*
>> Globus Project, *www.globus.org*
>> Home Phoneline Networking Alliance, *www.homepna.org*
>> HomePlug Powerline Alliance, *www.homeplug.org*
>> IBM Deep Blue, *www.research.ibm.com/deepblue/*
>> IBM E-Business On Demand, *http://www-1.ibm.com/services/ondemand/index_flash.html*
>> Inxight, *http://www.inxight.com*
>> IXI Mobile, *www.ixi.com*
>> Microsoft Research, *http://research.Microsoft.com*
>> M.I.T. Technology Review, "A.I. Reboots," Michael Hiltzik, March 2002, *http://www.technologyreview.com/articles/hiltzik0302.asp*
>> M.I.T. Technology Review, "The Next Computer Interface," Claire Tristram, December 2001, *http://www.technologyreview.com/articles/tristram1201.asp*
>> Open Grid Services Architecture, *http://www.globus.org/ogsa/*
>> Power Line Networking, Scientific American, "The Network in Every Room," W. Wyatt Gibbs, February 2002
>> Scopeware, *http://www.scopeware.com*
>> Smart Fuel Cell GmbH, *http://www.smartfuelcell.com*
>> Sun Grid Engine Software, *http://wwws.sun.com/software/gridware/*
>> Wireless Ethernet Compatibility Alliance, *www.wi-fi.org*

# Chapter 10

>> *"This is not the end, it is not even the beginning of the end. But it is, perhaps, the end of the beginning."*—Sir Winston Churchill
Sir Winston Churchill (1874–1965), Speech in November 1942, The Quotations Page, *http://www.quotationspage.com*

# Index

# About The Author

NICHOLAS D. EVANS is a Director within the Emerging Technology Solutions practice of one of the world's leading business advisors and systems integrators. A widely recognized e-business consultant, speaker, and author, Evans has published over 100 articles for publications ranging from *The Financial Times* to *Internet Week*. His books include *Business Agility: Strategies for Gaining Competitive Advantage through Mobile Business Solutions* (Financial Times Prentice Hall).

Evans was formerly National Technical Director for e-business at PricewaterhouseCoopers' Global Software Solutions Center. He co-founded the National Internet Practice for Coopers & Lybrand in 1997. Evans' clients have included 3M, AT&T, Abbott Labs, American Airlines, American Family Insurance, Best Buy, BP Amoco, Compaq, Conoco, First USA, Intel, Johnson & Johnson, Kodak, Major League Baseball, Schering Plough, SunTrust Bank, Texaco, Van Waters and Rogers, and many others.

Evans holds a B.Sc.(Hons) and M.Sc. from Southampton University in England. He is a frequent advisor to the venture capital community and serves on several advisory boards.

Readers who would like to correspond with the author can contact him at *ndevans@hotmail.com*.

# 8 reasons why you should read the Financial Times for 4 weeks RISK-FREE!

To help you stay current with significant
developments in the world economy ...
and to assist you to make informed business
decisions — the Financial Times brings you:

**❶** Fast, meaningful overviews of international affairs ... plus daily briefings on major world news.

**❷** Perceptive coverage of economic, business, financial and political developments with special focus on emerging markets.

**❸** More international business news than any other publication.

**❹** Sophisticated financial analysis and commentary on world market activity plus stock quotes from over 30 countries.

**❺** Reports on international companies and a section on global investing.

**❻** Specialized pages on management, marketing, advertising and technological innovations from all parts of the world.

**❼** Highly valued single-topic special reports (over 200 annually) on countries, industries, investment opportunities, technology and more.

**❽** The Saturday Weekend FT section — a globetrotter's guide to leisure-time activities around the world: the arts, fine dining, travel, sports and more.

# The *Financial Times* delivers a world of business news.

## Use the Risk-Free Trial Voucher below!

To stay ahead in today's business world you need to be well-informed on a daily basis. And not just on the national level. You need a news source that closely monitors the entire world of business, and then delivers it in a concise, quick-read format.

With the *Financial Times* you get the major stories from every region of the world. Reports found nowhere else. You get business, management, politics, economics, technology and more.

Now you can try the *Financial Times* for 4 weeks, absolutely risk free. And better yet, if you wish to continue receiving the *Financial Times* you'll get great savings off the regular subscription rate. Just use the voucher below.